T0319623

7 Roles to Create Sustainable Success

CAROLA WIJDOOGEN

A PRACTICAL GUIDE FOR SUSTAINABILITY AND CSR PROFESSIONALS

7 Roles for Sustainable Success is printed in the Netherlands by Wilco Printers, who themselves aim to work with respect for the environment, their employees and customers (ISO 14001 certified). The heat generated by the printing process is reused to warm their building. The company is compensating all production, transport and employee commuting, to neutralize their CO_2 emissions to zero. In addition, new trees have been planted by Land Life Company to compensate for the paper and the CO_2 emissions to get this book to you. See the trees we planted for this book here: www.landlifecompany.com. Land Life Company is a tech-driven reforestation company that restores degraded land in Southern Europe, the US and Australia.

In order to extend the lifetime and positive impact of the book, we used good quality design: please share or resell the book after reading. And at the end of the book's lifetime, please recycle.

Cover design and layout: Justus Bottenheft
Editing: Selese Roche, Jodi van Oudheusden-Peita
Illustrations: Shirley Warlich, www.visenchips.nl

© 2020 Carola Wijdoogen and
Sustainability University Foundation Amsterdam

ISBN 978-90-829497-4-2
ISBN E-book 978-90-829497-5-9

Table of Contents

FIGURE O.1 **Roles of a sustainability professional** (numbers refer to pages of chapters)

For Sarah and Juliet

Speeding up transitions: new mindset, skills and competencies

The transitions we're currently experiencing are of such magnitude that "business as usual" is no longer an option. The Covid-19 outbreak dramatically exposes the vulnerability of our vital systems and magnifies the vulnerability of vulnerable individuals in our societies. In times of uncertainty, listening to the needs of all kinds of individuals is no longer a "nice to have" (if it ever was…) but a "need to have." Digitalization is radically changing the way we interact, share and produce. The energy transition requires us to question commonly held beliefs about abundance and scarcity, fundamentally rethink business models and processes and co-create innovative solutions. With the roles of government, companies, societal players and citizens shifting, the days when ideas could be developed in ivory towers are definitely gone.

Sustainability and CSR professionals are crucial change agents who can help shape and speed up these transitions. Fulfilling this important role requires the right mindset, skills and competencies. It is far less romantic and definitely way more complicated than it sounds but, in the end, far more satisfying than many of the traditional roles. At its core, it demands a strong belief that change is not only possible but urgent and non-negotiable. If you do not truly believe in what you do, why should others follow you? And because of the scope of the changes needed, you cannot do this alone. Partnership based on equality, real dialogue and co-creation are preconditions for success. Obtaining what you want is not about selling a slick story but about creating a shared mission and narrative with unexpected experts, as well as the usual suspects.

These approaches are about asking the right questions rather than receiving definitive answers. What was said and what wasn't? And what was said between the lines? The late physicist David Bohm wrote about dialogue:

> *"Free dialogue may well be one of the most effective ways of investigating the crises facing society and indeed the whole of human nature and consciousness today."*

Meandering processes of developing shared plans and ambitious missions are, by definition, chaotic. So linear processes and hierarchical reporting lines generally do not apply. Change agents create the paths and connections necessary to free up the way for the incremental steps that will lead to systemic change. Paradoxically, working with so many others to serve a big goal can feel lonely. So, what do you, as a professional, need to be happy and effective in such a dynamic environment? Whether you think independently, are constructively disruptive and harmoniously persistent, is a personal choice. But giving up is not an option and self-reflection and humor are a must in order to survive.

The remarkable Carola Wijdoogen knows firsthand what it takes to be professionally effective and personally aligned with the work she undertakes in sustainability and CSR. In this survival guide, she generously shares her rich experiences and insights. It can thus help those who not only want to speed up transitions but also want to practice these principles in their everyday lives.

HRH PRINCESS LAURENTIEN OF THE NETHERLANDS, AUTHOR, FOUNDER
READING & WRITING FOUNDATION, MISSING CHAPTER FOUNDATION,
NUMBER 5 FOUNDATION

Business leadership for sustainable development

W e live in a volatile world. Even though life — before COVID-19 — was a better experience for more people than it has been at any time in history, it is clear now that the system simply has not been functioning effectively — socially, politically, environmentally and economically.

Through shocks like COVID-19, which has caught us all woefully unprepared and has been stress-testing the system dramatically, it has become apparent that business as usual is out of question and that we need to press hard on creating a more sustainable long-term world for our people and planet, with improved risk awareness and resilience in our supply chains, operations and business models. With social inequality sadly being on a steep rise and bigger shocks than the Corona crisis yet to come, including climate change, we should better be prepared next time.

Now is a pivotal moment for business to lead the way in achieving a world where more than nine billion people have a decent quality of life within the boundaries of our planet by 2050; if we miss this opportunity, we will have failed. In 2015, both the Paris Agreement and the Sustainable Development Goals (SDGs) gave us internationally agreed frameworks we can use for transforming systems. Put simply, they emphasize the need for a deep change in the way our economies work, and in the way our energy, mobility, urbanization, food and social systems contribute to planetary and societal well-being. In particular, the SDGs provide us with a global agenda that can help stimulate action from all sectors that benefit both people and the planet.

For companies, there is a clear business case for engaging with the SDGs. Companies that understand (and improve) their SDG impacts are better placed to manage operational, regulatory and reputational risks. On the path to 2030, unlocking potentially historic market opportunities can yield at least USD $12 trillion in business value, while generating up to 380 million jobs, as well as consolidating an enduring license to operate.

At the World Business Council for Sustainable Development (WBCSD), we have been working twenty-five years, with over two hundred member-companies from across the globe, to develop practical solutions to accomplish this. We advocate that business has a leading role to play as the world embarks upon this vital journey. In fact, forward-looking companies are not only integrating sustainability at the core of their strategy, decision-making and disclosures, as long-standing masters of innovation, they are also ideally positioned to become the implementation partner of choice in capturing opportunities across systems change. The time has now come for accelerating the transition to a sustainable world where business and the capital markets contribute to a flourishing society and where managing a company within the boundaries of the planet is the norm.

At the core, corporate sustainability leaders are key to the achievement of these goals; they create a meaningful contribution and have a positive impact, both for their companies and for society at large. In order to effectively translate sustainability goals into action and success, companies need sustainability professionals equipped with the necessary skills. I am pleased that this book is helping accelerate sustainable development by providing the tools for professionals on their sustainability journey.

The result will be a world that is better for everyone — including businesses, which cannot survive in a society and planet that fails.

PETER BAKKER, PRESIDENT AND CEO OF THE WORLD BUSINESS COUNCIL FOR SUSTAINABLE DEVELOPMENT (WBCSD). MR. BAKKER HAS LED WBCSD — A GLOBAL, CEO-LED ORGANIZATION OF OVER 200 LEADING BUSINESSES WORKING TOGETHER TO ACCELERATE THE TRANSITION TO A SUSTAINABLE WORLD — SINCE 2012.

The challenges we face are enormous. I have seen with my own eyes that the ice in the Arctic is melting faster than expected and our natural "air-conditioning" is disappearing. Plastic pollution in the oceans is increasing and plastic micro debris is likely to enter our food chain. The loss of nature is ongoing. Environmental disruption is increasing our vulnerability to pandemics that threaten our health, well-being, and economy. In order to protect our planet and create a sustainable future, we need to speed up and accelerate our transition to an inclusive, fossil-free and circular economy.

We have a hard task ahead, but we should not be discouraged by the magnitude of the challenge. Gradually, we are getting to know what needs to be done and we — at least most of us — even agree that action needs to be taken. The Paris Climate Convention and the UN Sustainable Development Goals have been signed and new ways of thinking about economic growth, like the Doughnut Economy, have been introduced.

A growing number of companies aim to play an important role in this transition. They see not only challenges but also opportunities and seek ways to possibly turn the tide. To support their transition to sustainable business, they often appoint a Chief Sustainability Officer (CSO) or a Corporate Social Responsibility (CSR) manager.

In 2010, I became the first Chief Sustainability Officer for the Dutch Railway (NS). The position was not only new to NS, it was also new to me. Fortunately, at that time there were several CSOs already doing a great job in similar organizations. To learn what a CSO does, I started interviewing them.

What makes a Chief Sustainability Officer effective? Most of the CSOs answered that it takes perseverance — dealing with ups and downs — and learning by trial and error to find out what is effective. As no company and no situation are alike, a one-size-fits-all solution does not exist. At the same time, I found that, although companies and situations might vary, the 7 different Roles of a CSO — based on scientific research — appears to be the same for every sustainability professional around the world. An effective CSO knows how and when which role is needed, and s(he) can alternate the different roles if the situation requires it.

From these peers, I also learned that there is no such thing as a "sustainability profession." Our jobs are temporary, since the assignment of a CSO is to embed sustainability in all processes and activities of a company or an organization. So, the sooner we — as CSOs — become redundant, the better.

Nine years later however, the first generation of sustainability professionals is still here and the challenges we face are more complex and more urgent than ever. As a consequence, the need for more effective corporate sustainability leaders, who can speed up the transition, is growing.

Most of us learn the job by listening and exchanging information with our peers. When I was awarded the title of Dutch CSO of the Year, I made it my goal to stimulate peer-to-peer learning for sustainability professionals to boost their impact around the world.

With *7 Roles to Create Sustainable Success*, I want to contribute to that goal. I wrote it with my own experiences in mind, using the structure of the 7 Roles. What did it take to make NS the world's first railway company with 100% wind-powered trains? Which roles did I use, when and how? In addition, the book draws upon the experiences and best practices of many other CSOs and sustainability professionals. Their willingness to help stems from the "deeper drive" that unites us: accelerating sustainability in business.

7 Roles to Create Sustainable Success is just one step in my journey to stimulate peer-to-peer learning between corporate sustainability leaders around the world. It covers only a fragment of the existing know-how among CSOs. I hope that it will also inspire other (former) CSOs to share their knowledge and join the global peer-to-peer learning platform of the Sustainability University Foundation[1], a co-founded social enterprise with the purpose of accelerating sustainability in business!

Introduction

What is the added value of a Chief Sustainability Officer (CSO) or Corporate Social Responsibility (CSR) manager for a company? And what kind of work is (s)he supposed to do in a company? When is a CSO, sustainability or CSR manager effective in his or her job? The answers to these questions are described in this book on the basis of the 7 Roles that are needed to fully embed sustainability or corporate social responsibility in a company.

Each role is different and adds specific value to the embedding process in the company (Figure 1.1). The roles are based on the scientific research of the competencies of CSO or CSR managers of Eghe Osagie[2], in which she describes the Networker, Strategist, Coordinator, Stimulator, Mentor and Monitor roles. After conducting applied research among sustainability professionals, three amendments to her findings were made:

- *The Coordinator role* — based on the formal governance of a company — is expanded with the Initiator role, because starting a project or activity yourself and showing how changes can been made often works as a catalyst
- *The Stimulator role* is expanded with the Connector role, because the CSO — as a sustainability ambassador without formal influence — not only stimulates change but also creates new connections with a multidisciplinary cross-company approach
- *The Innovator role* is added, since driving relevant innovations is essential for achieving the sustainability goals and for realizing new sustainable business models.

CSO or CSR managers should not take on the execution or production roles of a company. In *7 Roles to Create Sustainable Success*, I link each of the 7 Roles with the specific CSR or sustainability activities that need to be done within a role, based on the practical experience of many CSOs or CSR managers.

One could view this list of roles and CSR activities as a chronological and continuous step-by-step plan. Opinions vary on the correct order in which to take

FIGURE 1.1 **Short overview of the roles of a sustainability professional**

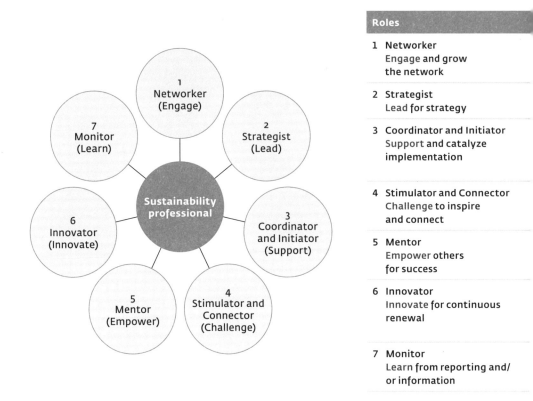

Roles

1 Networker
   Engage and grow
   the network

2 Strategist
   Lead for strategy

3 Coordinator and Initiator
   Support and catalyze
   implementation

4 Stimulator and Connector
   Challenge to inspire
   and connect

5 Mentor
   Empower others
   for success

6 Innovator
   Innovate for continuous
   renewal

7 Monitor
   Learn from reporting and/
   or information

the steps, but it seems logical to start with the Strategic role. Then you are focusing on the "why" of sustainable entrepreneurship or CSR and the creation of a vision and (integrated) strategy. The interpretation of the "why" largely determines the focus of your work as a CSR or sustainability manager. But starting with the Monitor role can also be effective because, in that role, you can determine your starting point by making clear what has already happened in the field of CSR or sustainability. My experience, however, is that practice is not always reflected in a step-by-step plan. I myself have followed a different order and I have often been busy with different activities and roles at the same time.

Some activities are linked to more than one role. In this book, I describe a role by showing the typical key activities that need to be executed, although these might be useful for other roles as well. So, for example, I show the role of the Networker by describing the practice of involving stakeholders. However, by involving stakeholders in your Network role, you are also creating internal support for sustainability (Stimulator role) by bringing questions

Description of the role
Create and maintain networks around the sustainability field and the organization's sustainability program. Representing the company and its program in meetings with external *stakeholders*, peers and other parties. This is all about engaging the relevant stakeholders.
Develop the sustainability strategy and integrate this into the overall strategy of the organization. This is all about creating a *vision and mission*.
Support people in other departments in the organization to implement the sustainability strategy **using the governance/organizational structure**. You work with many others to create an (integrated) *plan, to embed* it into the organization and to set things in motion. Initially it might include starting up iconic projects yourself.
Act as a sustainability ambassador, inspiring (outside-in) and activating others to integrate sustainability goals into tasks, usually **without formal influence**. This is all about *generating support* within the organization.
On an individual functional level: advise, inform and train colleagues, to enable them to achieve the sustainability goals. This is all about *translating sustainability to the daily reality of the workplace* of each team.
Initiating and guiding innovation processes, so that ideas and innovations can come to life and lead to implementation of sustainable business models, products and services. This role is all about embedding sustainability in innovation processes and *initiating and coaching innovation projects*.
In the monitoring role, you monitor, report and evaluate the progress of the sustainability goals and the related development of the organization. You collect, interpret and act upon relevant information. This role is all about (proactively) *measurement, reporting and improvement*.

from outside into your organization. And in your Network role, you are not only involved with stakeholders, you are also building networks of peers to obtain ideas for your innovative processes.

The classification of roles and activities fits well with my own duties and that of various fellow CSO and CSR managers and professionals in medium to large organizations. During my research, I found that the 7 Roles are recognized in different parts of the world; however, the definition and maturity of sustainability or CSR differ substantially. As the former West Africa CSR Director of SIFCA group Franck Eba states:

"You have to take different culture into account. CSR must adapt to the economic, social, political, cultural and environmental realities of the countries where it will be implemented."

Differences might decrease in the coming years, when international organizations and multinationals will continue to play an important role in setting the "sustainability agenda" globally.

Every company has its own sustainability journey. For a service provider without an innovation department, the role of the sustainability manager is different from the role in a manufacturing company with its own innovation team. Additionally, the roles and activities of the sustainability manager (or team) can change as sustainability is integrated more deeply into the organization. In an organization that is just starting its sustainability journey, you are likely to be the first sustainability manager. The Coordinator & Initiator roles will probably be your dominant roles, focusing on initiating projects and mapping what is in place already. When sustainability is integrated into the vision, the strategy and the innovation process, the CSR or sustainability manager will then focus more on challenging the organization to raise the bar and on driving breakthrough innovations. Some roles, like the Monitor role, might be taken by other departments. Eventually all 7 Roles will have to find an "owner" in the organization.

The everyday practice is different for every CSO, CSR or sustainability professional. That also makes the job interesting: not so easy to define!

What's in a name?

In this book, sustainability and CSR (social responsibility) will be used interchangeably, unless the context requires a precise interpretation of the difference between the two terms. I often use sustainability, because it is in line with UN definitions and covers the overall social impact of companies. The same holds for organization and company, or any other entity that engages in business. Although I often use the CSO (Chief Sustainability Officer) as the "main character" in the book, the 7 Roles also apply to other sustainability or CSR job levels, such as sustainability managers or project managers in divisions, staff and sustainability teams.

My journey

Throughout the book I will share my experiences and practices of my journey as a CSO of NS. In order to understand the context of these examples, I will first give you a short introduction to the company NS.

NS is a train operating company for passenger travel. It concentrates primarily on improving operational performance on the railways, supported by activities that include bicycle facilities, stations and improving the door-to-door journey, together with other public transport partners. It has 36,600

FIGURE 1.2 **Still of video with CEO Roger van Boxtel**

staff, yearly revenues of €5.9 billion, 89% of which comes from passenger transport. It is based in the Netherlands, was founded in 1837 and has one shareholder, the Dutch state. To many stakeholders, customer satisfaction, safety and punctuality are more important than the financial position. In the Netherlands, the State Secretary for Infrastructure and Water Management awarded NS the main rail transport franchise for a term of ten years to 2025. Another important stakeholder is ProRail, the network operator (part of the Ministry) that takes care of the national railway network infrastructure and allocates rail capacity. NS also operates franchises in Germany and the UK in order to — like other major European state railway companies — prepare for possible further deregulation of the European rail market.

To illustrate my journey to make NS the most sustainable railway company in the world, I will frequently refer to the major milestone, that all electric trains in the Netherlands have been running on 100% wind power since January 1st 2017. The Netherlands is believed to be the first country in the world to do this, which became world news when it was communicated by Roger van Boxtel, CEO of the NS in a very unusual way: he was tied to a windmill that was running on wind power as well. Figure 1.2 shows the still of the video. People often ask me, "how did you persuade your CEO to do this?" The answer can be found in this book.

Structure of the book

7 Roles to Create Sustainable Success can be read from cover to cover, or you can focus on specific sections if you have questions about certain issues or roles. Every sustainability manager's job is different: there is no fixed set of roles or activities that applies to all. Sustainability managers or professionals who fulfill only one or a few of the 7 Roles can easily find the roles or activities relevant to them.

In Chapters 2 to 8 consecutively, I describe the 7 Roles, explaining their deployment by describing the key activities linked to each role. I have indicated what I have done in practice, whether or not based on existing models and frameworks. I supplement each chapter with practices of other CSOs or experts and I end each chapter with a list of tips I have collected.

In Chapter 9, I describe the dynamics of the roles and how they can be deployed among others through an interview with Kate Raworth. First thoughts about the future of the sustainability team are shared by other experts. In Chapter 10, I describe which competencies a CSO needs most to be effective in relation to his or her roles and context. These chapters are at the end of the book because of the necessary references to Chapters 2 to 8. To get a better insight into the relevant roles and competencies for your own position, Chapters 9 and 10 can also be read first.

For the sake of legibility, the number of endnotes regarding literature and other sources has been limited in the chapters. The list of sources at the back is more extensive and also contains links to a number of relevant websites.

The Networker

*"Networks are defined equally by the nodes
and the holes in between them."*

PETER EVERSMAN, ASSOCIATE PROFESSOR OF THEATER STUDIES, UNIVERSITY OF AMSTERDAM

Networking is a key component of the CSO's role. This means maintaining relationships with external parties, creating connections and recognizing and shaping collaboration opportunities. You represent the sustainability profession and your company at external events or in external meetings, like a stakeholder dialogue. You build a network of peers who meet together and learn from each other. And usually you are responsible for the communications on the sustainability results of your organization, which includes speaking engagements.

The Network role is indispensable for stakeholder engagement. This chapter outlines stakeholder engagement activities and explains the related tasks for which a CSO or sustainability manager is responsible. This is highly dependent on how stakeholder engagement in an organization is structured. If stakeholders are already engaged and relationships are in place, then activities of a CSO include collecting and structuring sustainability-related information from existing stakeholder relationships. If nothing is in place or sustainability-related stakeholders such as non-governmental organizations (NGOs) are not engaged, then activities include organizing engagement from sustainability-related stakeholders.

Diane Holdorf (now Managing Director Food & Nature, WBCSD, formerly CSO and VP of environmental stewardship, health and safety of Kellogg Company):

"Key to the commitment of responsibly sourced palm oil is the power of dialogue, engaging stakeholders and benchmarking to promote changes within the industry."

When many stakeholder engagement activities already exist within the organization, the Network role is combined with the Coordinator role. In that case, the CSO or sustainability manager's main task regarding stakeholder engagement is to map and further develop the information collected. In short, the focus then is to integrate sustainability deeper into existing stakeholder processes.

2.1 Stakeholder engagement

Corporate responsibility or sustainability management is a continuous process. Together with stakeholders, companies structure the content of this process. stakeholders share what their sustainability interests are and how they perceive the company's economic, social and environmental value creation process. Engaging the stakeholders is, therefore, both an important and a complex condition to give direction and meaning to corporate sustainability and/or social responsibility.

Who are the stakeholders, actually? A broad definition is recommended: all internal and external people on whom your products or services have a significant impact and whose activities — in turn — can have a major influence on a company's performance. This includes clients, communities,

FIGURE 2.1 **Stakeholder diversity**

shareholders, politicians, government officials, suppliers, employees and civil society organizations, like NGOs.

Stakeholder interests can be expressed and served in different ways, either through individuals and organizations, but also through market research and international frameworks. There is a wide range of different engagement processes, including monitoring, consulting, negotiations, collaboration informing and active engagement.

Stakeholder interests will not always be aligned. They can conflict with each other, with the interests of the company and even with society at large. This causes dilemmas for companies. Sometimes, such dilemmas can move into the public domain, where media, politics and others join the conversation about the dilemma.

Actively engaging stakeholders does not simply help to give direction, it also helps to generate support for the organization and its CSR or sustainability strategy. It can even inspire a new social purpose for a company, as highlighted by Harriet Hentges, who was previously Senior Director of stakeholder Engagement at Walmart.

> *"The combination of the impact of Katrina and NGOs emphasizing the positive impact Walmart could have in solving common social problems, made the CEO realize that he could do so much good. That is when he decided to set sustainable goals for Walmart."*

Stakeholders influence a company's strategy in terms of how it can achieve its mission as well as in the daily course of events. Stakeholders have direct or indirect interests and will respond when these interests are affected. To ensure this influence is a positive one when facing dilemmas, it is vital to be proactive and transparent during discussions. In short, for any company, it is important to take stakeholders into account and to involve them proactively. For the CSO or CSR manager, it is therefore of great interest to build a strong network and to organize the inclusion of relevant stakeholders and their social interests.

You can organize stakeholder engagement by looking at your organization in two ways:
- What forms of regular contact already exists with your stakeholders? Through which processes?
- Which stakeholders are not yet engaged? How can you structure their engagement?

In any company, a process is usually already in place to engage market-related stakeholders that influence a company's core activities, such as clients, shareholders and core suppliers. Each department maintains its own relationships with its key stakeholders. As CSO or CSR manager, you can then insert sustainability topics into existing processes like client surveys, user panels or account management. There is also usually something in place to involve staff, like the employee-satisfaction survey or a worker council. Again, as CSO or CSR manager, you can request adding sustainability topics or questions to such surveys or agendas.

For the sustainability stakeholders that are not yet engaged, like NGOs or governments, first consider which department should build and maintain such a relationship. You can try to organize the involvement of this department, but you may have to initially develop the relationship yourself.

Companies with a longer history of stakeholder engagement usually hold (bi)annual central stakeholder dialogues. All stakeholders are invited to join and, as a group, discuss the results, ambitions and strategies of the company. These stakeholder dialogues are very valuable, not in the least because, through conversation, stakeholders are better able to calibrate the importance of their own interests. As CSO or CSR manager, you ensure that the stakeholders with strong sustainability interests are well represented.

For your own company, you can map the different stakeholders and determine how you want to engage with them. There are several roadmaps available, such as the GRI guidelines, ISO 26000 and local CSR guidelines.

It is important to conduct the stakeholder analysis together with senior management and colleagues who already have a relationship with various stakeholders. This helps you generate fundamental insights into who is engaged already and how, and whether this is something more structural or ad hoc. Capture the outcome of the stakeholder mapping in a policy document signed off by senior management.

Networking

A CSO or CSR manager represents the company at external events or in external meetings, not only at stakeholder dialogues, but also at other venues. Networking serves many purposes: finding partners in your sector or supply chain with whom to cooperate or innovate. Examples of this can be found in Chapter 7 in my discussions on the Innovator role. Learning from your peers is common practice when learning on the job as a sustainability professional. A network of peers to meet with and learn from is, therefore, crucial in developing know-how and gathering best practices.

There are many networks that a CSO can join: sector, product-specific or more general, national or international, like the World Business Council for Sustainable development (WBCSD). Some networks are free of charge or requirements, others are not. A proactive and careful selection of added value of a network for you or your company's goals is important, since time and resources are always limited. Ask the advice of your peers to find out what network would serve your purpose best, although you may eventually have to build a new network for a specific purpose or goal, such as a system change in your sector. Also, you might want to invite other colleagues, like procurement professionals, to this network to make use of their know-how or share their best practice.

At venues or events, which are often organized by networks, a CSO or CSR manager is usually responsible for communicating about the sustainability results of his or her organization, which includes speaking engagements. Chapter 5, which discusses the Stimulator role, gives insights on how to communicate in an effective way, including the selection of the most appropriate speaker, which could be a person other than yourself.

2.2 Stakeholder engagement in practice

One of the lessons learned by CSOs or CSR managers is that stakeholder engagement should be about building relationships and acting on issues and not about endless lists of issues and stakeholders.

> *"I do not believe in B2B or B2C, we are of*
> *course all B2S. Business to Society."*
> WINEKE HAAGSMA (DIRECTOR CORPORATE SUSTAINABILITY PWC THE NETHERLANDS & EMEA)

Stakeholder engagement is all about people, relationships, and communications. Dialogue takes place between people rather than between organizations. Mutual fears, fueled by opinions about each other, usually decrease in personal conversations and through a better understanding of each other's perspectives. Truly opening your door by inviting stakeholders for a working visit in order to really understand your business processes can positively trigger the spirit of partnership.

Being transparent, building relationships and opening the door seem to be repetitive themes in "best practices" for the Networker, even when it is your experience that a specific stakeholder might be out there, "to get you".

It takes courage to be transparent, openly discuss or even publish a company's conflict of interest. And, it takes courage to be transparent about how the interests of different stakeholders are weighed. It is crucial to be explicit about what a stakeholder can and cannot expect and to provide feedback. This can take many forms, including small things like sending participants a summary of a dialogue or conversation and big things like an invitation to work together to find solutions.

As a state-owned public transportation company, NS influences many stakeholders and vice versa. The organization is set up according to our societal role, following formal consultation and collaboration structures with our stakeholders. At NS, we actively follow relevant developments and regularly conduct research on the impact of our operational activities (Figure 2.2) on different stakeholders.

FIGURE 2.2 **NS inputs and impacts (annual report 2018)**

Whether we like it or not, NS is a regular topic for public debate, which is usually intensely covered by the Dutch media. An annual media analysis helps to understand the impact NS has on society. Therefore, this is also included in our stakeholder analysis.

Guidelines for sustainability reporting usually link stakeholder engagement to the selection of important (or material) topics. The way in which these guidelines structure the engagement of stakeholders with the company's activity, strategy and reporting, provides useful guidance to set up processes for stakeholder engagement. This section of the chapter outlines the practical example of the stakeholder engagement process of NS along the domains:

- Stakeholder inclusiveness — who influences us and whom do we influence? (who)
- Materiality — which themes are important for us and our stakeholders? (what)
- Responsiveness — how do we respond to material issues which are important to us and our stakeholders? (how)

Stakeholder inclusiveness

On which stakeholders does NS have an influence and vice versa? We began to address this by mapping the stakeholders with whom consultation structures and processes already exist. To this, we then added specific sustainability-related organizations. To prioritize the list of stakeholders, we plotted them in a matrix, with the impact of NS on stakeholders on one axis, and the ability for stakeholders to influence NS on the other axis, as shown in Figure 2.3. The stakeholder matrix also includes the variety of processes used to engage the different types of stakeholders.

Concerning the most important stakeholders where the mutual influence is large, you want to collaborate on value creation: you may even want to let them influence the direction of the company. You try to work with clients by asking their opinions in client research, asking for input in client panels, and by sharing ideas for new products and policies with them early on. In the case of NS, the latter is done with associations of public-transport users. Employee interests are represented through the works council and employee surveys. Other stakeholders, such as policy makers, are involved through regular meetings and by working in joint project teams.

Suppliers can have a large influence on a company, but that same company may not always impact them to the same extent. In that case, account management plays an important role to inform, consult and involve them.

FIGURE 2.3 **NS stakeholder matrix**

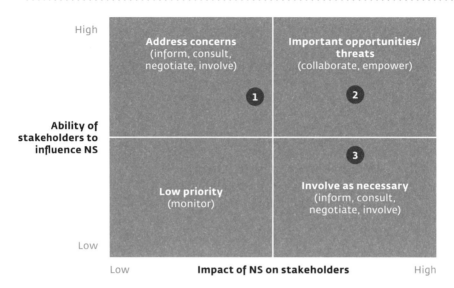

1 Suppliers
2 Clients, network operator ProRail, policy makers/government, employees
3 NGOs

However, some NGOs and suppliers offer such a wealth of opportunities (for example, as a source of innovations that can help your company achieve its goals), that the engagement takes a much more intense shape, such as collaboration.

Initially, NS did not have a structured engagement format with NGOs. This was changed by inviting them to take part in the central stakeholder dialogue, by consulting them in procurement processes and by asking them to collaborate on relevant activities.

Bob Langert (former VP Sustainability of McDonalds), explains how to choose a partner (NGO) in his book, The Battle to Do Good. It is one of many lessons he learned as a Networker:

> *"Do not pick a patsy but choose a partner that will challenge your organization. Evaluate partnership choices on a scale of 1-10, with 1 meaning corporate friendly and 10 meaning very radical. Work with NGOs in the 5-7 range, who are independent, credible, collaborative and knowledgeable about business and market forces; and practical rather than dogmatic."*

He adds that you should give up total control and invite this truly independent NGO into your business.

In my role as CSO, I also had a permanent role in proactively translating the interests of sustainability-related stakeholders (such as NGOs) towards the company. However I became redundant as their only point of contact in the organization. Increasingly, they found their own way to senior leadership and other management to provide their input or feedback.

Materiality

With your stakeholders, you want to engage in conversations about topics that matter to both parties. Companies with existing stakeholder relationships often already know what the current topics are and (hopefully) take them into consideration when carrying out their operational activities. Although current topics might be known, it is very interesting to also share with your stakeholders the topics that you envision becoming more important in the years to come. This is something to included explicitly in a (central) stakeholder dialogue.

To guide the discussion on topics for the future, you can use lists of relevant societal issues, such as the Sustainable Development Goals agreed within the United Nations or the Principles of the United Nations Global Compact. In the first central stakeholder dialogue for NS, I not only added NGOs to the list of stakeholders, but also relevant societal issues to the long list of potential material topics to discuss.

A materiality matrix is a useful tool to generate an overview of topics and to prioritize them on importance and impact. In the matrix, the interests of the stakeholders are plotted against the impact of your organization. To create such a materiality matrix for NS, I set up the first central stakeholder dialogues. These dialogues now take place every year or every other year. Meanwhile, the ownership for organizing the central stakeholder dialogue has been transferred to the communications & stakeholder management department.

During a central dialogue meeting, to which all relevant stakeholders are invited, a structured process is used to determine and prioritize the material topics. To note the outcome of this process, the presence of an independent third party is recommended. You may also opt to invite the accountant, who will assure the company's annual report to join the dialogue to understand how the materiality matrix was created.

FIGURE 2.4 **NS materiality matrix (annual report 2018)**

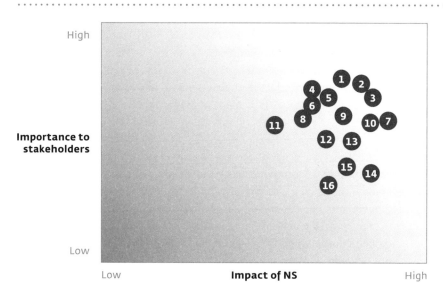

1 Reliability
2 Transparency (internal and external)
3 Customer satisfaction
4 Collaboration (internal and external)
5 Sustainability (internal and external)
6 Seamless door-to-door journeys
7 Integrity
8 Punctuality
9 Accessibility
10 Stations and facilities
11 Safety (including personal safety)
12 Innovation
13 Risk management
14 Financial position
15 Operations in Europe
16 An attractive and caring employer

Figure 2.4 represents the NS materiality matrix. This matrix is used to assess whether NS is focused on those topics that are most important for now and the future and to provide focus and scope for the report.

Nowadays you can also find standardized materiality maps such as the SASB materiality map® which identifies sustainability issues that are likely to affect the financial condition or operating performance of companies within an industry (https://www.sasb.org/) for a number of relevant dimensions.

Responsiveness

How do we respond to material issues that are important to us and our stakeholders? Again, there is a difference between existing processes around certain topics (such as reporting on train punctuality and improving related policies) and new processes that respond to stakeholders and integrate new topics into strategy. The role of the CSR manager or CSO can be quite substantial in this case. For me, the strong desire of stakeholders to base our energy supply on renewable energy was such a topic. For other topics, I hardly needed to be involved.

TABLE 2.1 **An example of NS's reporting on stakeholder dialogues**

· ·

	Nature of dialogue	Content of dialogue°	Effects of the dialogue on NS policy
Interest groups and NGOs (including employers)	Involvement, consultative for information	1, 2, 3, 4, 5, 6, 9, 11, 16 Encouraging sustainable mobility (via employers), contributing to climate agreement, next move for NS in energy transition, circular economy, social policy, making replacement bus service more sustainable, next step in promoting accessible train travel for people with visual, physical or hearing impairments	Including: • Making NS's own mobility policy more sustainable • Safeguard measures for encouraging sustainable mobility via employers in the climate agreement and other policies • Collaboration with 45 major employers in "Anders Reizen" coalition on implementation of measures to further sustainable mobility • Jobs created for people who are disadvantaged in the labor market • Investigation started into deployment of own assets for generating energy • Refining impact calculations for better investment decisions
Trade unions	Intensive involvement	4, 12, 16 Collective labor agreement, personal safety, pension plan, social plan, personal and social consequences of organizational changes, signs suggesting satisfaction or dissatisfaction among staff, employees' interests, long-term NS strategy	• Implementation of collective labor agreements 2017-2020 and resulting HR policy • Implementation of the social plan • Implementation of the pension plan • Implementation and evaluation of a packet of measures for personal safety and the Wage Tax (Implementation) Decree
Suppliers, subcontractors	Consulting and making acquaintances, negotiating conditions, making contract agreements, intensifying collaboration, innovation and development	5, 6, 7, 8, 9, 10, 11, 12, 13, 14, 15, 16 Sustainability, specifying, transparency, financial position, integrity, innovation, reliability, risk management, collaboration, intensification	• Achievement of CSR objectives (by making entire supply chain more sustainable) • Introduction of new products and services • Focus on more value creation for NS • Focus on reliability and availability of products and services for business-critical processes • More attention to compliance with legislation and regulations • Agree mutual expectations with suppliers • Introduce new suppliers • Encourage

° The numbers in the third column correspond to the numbering of the material issues in Figure 2.4

In NS's annual report, we publish an overview of our key stakeholders, the topics we have discussed with them and how we have responded to the outcomes of these discussions. Table 2.1 gives an example of this for a small selection of the stakeholders.

2.3 The learning Networker

Signaling issues early on

Even with a well-structured stakeholder dialogue process and effective networking — both with the intention of understanding what is going on in society — unexpected and new material issues can still emerge. They develop from so-called "early issues", which are either less clear or are more likely to manifest themselves in the future and have been overlooked by both the company and its stakeholders. Most likely, these topics are not part of the regular conversations, as these are more focused on current and urgent topics. Issues can also stay submerged because they do not (yet) have an owner or have a less well-organized stakeholder. An early issue — possibly triggered by a news item — can suddenly turn into a "hot" and material topic. An example of this is the recent change in what is considered socially acceptable behavior regarding corporate taxes. Whatever the cause, if issues are not recognized (in time), it can be very detrimental when they suddenly emerge and a quick-fix solution is sought under pressure; for example, due to negative news coverage.

The risk of unexpected material issues cannot be entirely eliminated; however, the following might reduce the risk and effects:

- Detect early issues under the surface by actively asking stakeholders. This is easier when you engage a limited number of stakeholders. Activist shareholders can often be the source of early issues.
- Search for early issues that can blow over from abroad or from other sectors. Find and appoint an owner for such issues locally so they can be discussed in more detail.
- When issues suddenly become urgent, do not fall into the trap of going for the quick solution but, first, assess its coherence with the company and material topics and weigh it against long-term interests.
- Transparently and proactively, show how interests and early issues of different stakeholders are taken into account in policy and decisions.

There are sound manuals to set up stakeholder policy and to determine material topics. But in reality, things can take a different course due to early issues that unexpectedly become material. By proactively organizing early-issue signaling in your Network role, you can make an important difference:

even more so, if brand and reputation are the primary business drivers when it comes down to sustainability or CSR.

The unattractive dialogue

There is always room for improvement in stakeholder dialogues. You want to avoid important stakeholders staying away from the table because they do not expect to get anything in return, or because there are too many dialogues or too few, or that the timing of a central stakeholder dialogue conflicts with other events. In addition, you run the risk that the demanding stakeholders engage while the satisfied stakeholders stay away. This latter group can raise interesting positive issues that you might also like to include.

In short, stakeholder engagement demands thorough planning, a comprehensive assessment of whom you want to engage with, what you want from the stakeholder dialogue and what you offer in return. Sometimes this requires personally getting in touch with specific stakeholders to emphasize the importance of their participation. To raise participation and engagement, you could consider the question: what's in it for them? And you could, for instance, hold your central stakeholder dialogue at a relevant conference, or invite an interesting speaker. Another way to create more continuous engagement is always to start each stakeholder dialogue with feedback on the most discussed topics of the previous dialogue.

Stakeholders might feel like they have a very instrumental role; for example, as a process step in the materiality analysis. Some stakeholders may feel neglected after they have participated. Even if you connect them to colleagues (as follow-up to a stakeholder dialogue), you cannot assume that these connections will automatically develop. You may have to accompany some of these connections within your organization. In that case, you are both a Networker and a Connector (which is covered in Chapter 5).

While there is always room for improvement in stakeholder engagement, there are also many things that are going well. An example of this was the first central stakeholder dialogue I organized for NS. Only ten stakeholders were present, including representatives of several Dutch Ministries, a client organization, network operator ProRail, the workers' council, NGOs and suppliers. By having them engage in a joint conversation about their different — and sometimes conflicting — interests, a shared sense of prioritization emerged for our material issues. Slowly, we became the audience to a dialogue among our most important stakeholders. This is how I discovered the value of having all your stakeholders discuss your organization and the issues all together.

The use of statements also proved very valuable in such conversations. Some issues hardly came up in regular contacts because they were going well, the focus often being placed on issues where there is room for improvement. This path is mistaken, as it leaves less time for things that are important and going well. The central stakeholder dialogue also helped us to determine the topics that are both material and going well.

Last but not least, for stakeholder engagement to be effective, it is essential to build rapport between people. I have invested time in engaging with the people that represent our stakeholders. I found that this goes beyond the job title and content, but is also about the ability to build mutual trust. I used to get quite agitated if an NGO would send an email to our CEO without my knowledge. Now I understand this is just part of the game. An angry reply to that email usually does not help: picking up the phone is preferable. In the end, you need each other to achieve your objectives, but the way each of you gets there might differ. To really understand each other takes time, personal contact and a willingness to listen (which often means to let go of your own convictions) and the ability to give up total control.

2.4 The successful Networker

Involving stakeholders

Anniek Mauser (Sustainability Director at Unilever Benelux) shares her journey as Networker:

"It is very tempting to manage by numbers, so you can show your stakeholders good results, clear progress and how serious you are on the issue. The real challenge however, and what in the end really engages your stakeholders, is to build a trusted relationship with them, based on true transparency and in which you show you have the courage to be vulnerable. In our sustainable palm oil journey, for example, using green palm certificates in the process as accelerator towards traceable sustainable certified palm oil was a key element. A couple of years ago we had to conclude that this route wasn't bringing the necessary acceleration towards traceable, sustainably produced, palm oil. To contribute to the overall sector transition, and our 100% traceable sustainable palm oil objective, we could more effectively invest this money in supporting palm oil smallholders and reforestation on the ground.

This resulted in a negative effect on the overall global sustainably sourced ingredients percentage we could report, so a tough discussion with stakeholders ensued. It was necessary to explain that the overall result is what matters and the route is a means not a goal. My experience is that, in the end, this is highly appreciated by your stakeholders."

Networks and multi-stakeholder platforms

Niels van Geenhuizen (Global Leader Sustainable Solutions of Arcadis) explains how his Network role is essential to creating new models of public-private co-operation needed to contribute to the SDGs:

"As Arcadis, we are a member of the WBCSD (World Business Council for Sustainable Development). This business network has enabled me to work with other companies in the program, Transforming Urban Mobility, reducing the carbon footprint and improving the quality of life in cities, with a focus on mobility. Arcadis is co-leading this program, because for us it is a win-win situation, creating new markets and insights for our business and contributing to the SDGs and our purpose; improving quality of life. And for me, as a CSO, it helps me to further embed sustainability in our core activities. And within the WBCSD — in my Network role I convinced other partners to join and set up a Corporate Mobility Pledge with companies and cities. With our technologies, but also as a big employer with a company mobility policy for our employees, companies like Arcadis have an important role to play in reducing the use of cars in cities around the globe."

Around 50% of passenger travel in a country or city is influenced by employer's policies because of a "system lock-in". For example, if you provide a company car, people will use it to commute, travel for business and for leisure. The same holds for the sustainable alternative: a free public transport card. For the latter, however, good public transport facilities in cities are needed. In the city of Lisbon, in October 2019, the first Corporate Sustainable Mobility Pledge was implemented. Together with certain companies, the city will develop several mobility hubs near the highways of the city, with good zero-emission public transport modes into the city. The companies promise to use those hubs and transport systems for their personnel. Niels concludes:

"I spent quite some time in my Network role in order to accomplish this, but it is absolutely worth it."

Renewable energy — wind for the trains — Network role

Stakeholders had very specific expectations of the role of NS in accomplishing (more) renewable energy for the Dutch trains. In my Network role, I involved them from the start and encouraged them to challenge us and the sources of renewable energy. They indicated the following expectations:

- As a major user of electricity, NS should take steps to make its energy more sustainable, without presenting the bill to its customers
- NS should become an active player in this field, not as a producer of renewable energy, but facilitating others to do so
- The sources of renewable energy must be clear and it must come from new facilities with clean technology. Stakeholders are increasingly critical of producers of renewable energy.

To supplement the central stakeholder dialogue, we conducted research with our most important stakeholder: the traveler. Figure 2.5 displays the most important outcomes of that research.

FIGURE 2.5 **Most important outcomes customer survey "renewable energy"**

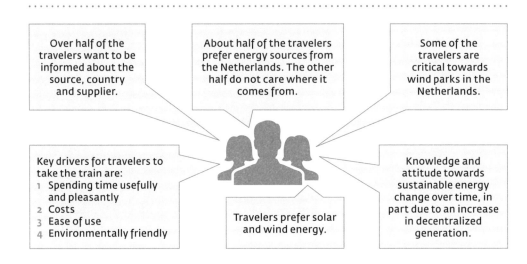

After setting our renewable energy targets, we asked our clients what they thought of making half our trains run on wind energy by 2015 and all of our trains by 2018. This was much appreciated by 85% of our clients. Eventually we reached our goal one year earlier, in 2017. In addition, the other train operating companies in the Netherlands were involved, so that all electric trains in the Netherlands could run on wind energy.

The contribution of NGOs was extremely important because they shared their expectations about the role of NS in the energy transition, their knowledge about truly renewable energy and supported us in our search for leveraging our impact in a sustainable way. NGOs were involved before, during and after the entire project to help us find the best way to approach this. In the beginning, the situation felt vulnerable because I did not know if we could live up to their (NGOs) expectations. After I shared this feeling with the NGOs, a very open dialogue arose. In my roles as Networker and Coordinator, I also kept my internal stakeholders aligned, so that we could inform the NGOs of our expectations and possibilities. Because of their reservations concerning the use of biomass, we specified the tender in such a way that our definitions were actually stricter than government policy and the government's definitions of renewable energy. Because of the transparent, high-involvement process, NGOs supported the project as a best practice (when asked).

Tips for Networkers

- Actively build or join a network that can help you achieve your goals. For example, by learning from your peers, sharing and finding best practices, building coalitions and/or engaging stakeholders.
- Have influential stakeholders engage in conversation with key people in your company to share how sustainable business can generate positive value for your organization. An example of such an influential stakeholder is the lead accountant, who has access to the boardroom.
- Engage stakeholders proactively. If there are no stakeholder engagement processes yet, first consider what you will do with their input before engaging them.
- If stakeholder engagement processes are in place, investigate how best to join these processes. Put sustainability topics on the agenda and add sustainability-related stakeholders; for example, by suggesting specific social topics and adding NGOs to the list of important stakeholders.
- Reduce fear of transparency within the organization. Highlight the benefits of sharing dilemmas in a joint stakeholder dialogue.
- Be aware that building and maintaining your network and engaging stakeholders requires a human touch. It is all about people, relationships and communications.
- Be honest about what stakeholders can and cannot expect from you and your company and admit if you do not have the answers (yet). Build a trusting relationship with them, based on true transparency and where you show you have the courage to be vulnerable.
- Stay focused on the long-term goal and if necessary, be tough in order to reach it.
- Ensure stakeholders reap some benefit if they engage. Make it attractive: avoid endless lists of issues and survey questions.
- Always make it clear what will be done with stakeholders' input. Provide feedback, for example, by means of a report.
- Allow stakeholders to influence the way in which your company defines and fulfils its social responsibility.
- Do not just pay attention to dissatisfied or angry stakeholders, but also actively seek out positive stakeholders to ensure that you generate a balanced view of your impact.
- Be alert to issues under the surface and early issues. Do not just rely on your own organization for information; discovering such issues often takes more effort and attention than you can provide in the regular stakeholder contact.
- Be aware that there might be relevant issues that do not (yet) have an owner. Search proactively for such issues by keeping up with trends and developments, for example, from other countries and industries.
- In the case that your sustainability report will be externally assured, do invite your accountant to the stakeholder dialogues focused on determining the material topics.

- Stakeholder engagement — as well as maintaining and building internal and external networks — is a continuous process that requires time and careful attention.
- Build a diverse network with various parties, points of view and backgrounds. This provides valuable insights into various viewpoints in society.
- When stakeholders have conflicting interests, bring them together for a joint conversation.
- Know how to choose your partners — pick those that are challenging but not radical — and show openness and commitment to the partnership.

The Strategist

"Look at the tiny mouse, such a sharp animal it is that would never entrust its life to just one little hole."

PLAUTUS (254-184 BC), ROMAN PLAYWRIGHT

As CSO or sustainability manager, you are responsible for the development of a sustainability strategy and (partially) for integrating this strategy into the overall strategy of the organization. You build sustainable business models and initiatives. Due to this strategic part of the role, you are viewed as a relevant business partner inside and outside the company.

"CSOs should realize that companies really have a big role to play. Next to being a participant, we need to be a change agent, allowing other (smaller) companies to follow our lead. Overcoming barriers by coming up with new products and solutions and finding new partners in other sectors."

BRIAN JANOUS (GENERAL MANAGER OF ENERGY AND SUSTAINABILITY AT MICROSOFT)

An important task in the Strategic role of the sustainability manager is creating a sustainable vision and mission and embedding this in the overall strategy. This chapter explores how CSOs or sustainability managers can take on this role by showing, for instance, how sustainability creates value for stakeholders and shareholders. It also highlights how having a vision and mission on sustainability advances the integration of sustainability in the organization, and with that, the role and influence of the sustainability manager. Conversely, the scope of the Strategic role is determined by the space you get within the organization to exert influence. Many sustainability managers who are new to the role indicate that the Strategic role is challenging for them; for example, because senior leadership does not (yet) regard the position as having a strategic input.

3.1 Sustainable value creation

What does a sustainability vision and mission entail? The vision describes how a company looks at (future) society and which role it wants to play within that society. What does your organization stand for, what are its fundamental values, what should be its contribution to society? This societal role is the normative basis upon which business can act responsibly. The mission makes that role concrete; it sets the point on the horizon that you want to reach. The strategy displays the way to get there and makes the vision of the future solid by attaching goals to the mission. What needs to be achieved in

FIGURE 3.1 **The Doughnut Economy (Kate Raworth)**

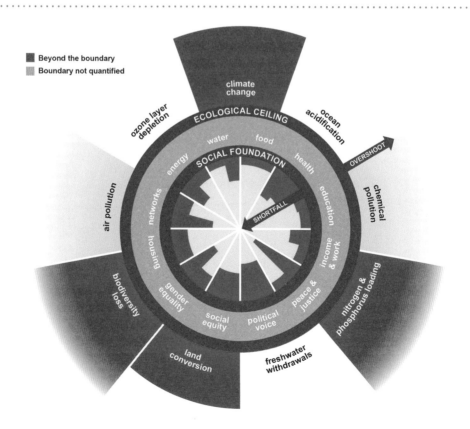

the desired situation? Many companies call the journey to achieving a vision and mission "the strategy process".

FIGURE 3.2 **The Natural Step "Back-casting"** (2018 | The Natural Step International | Registered in Sweden, EU | org.nr 802409-2358)

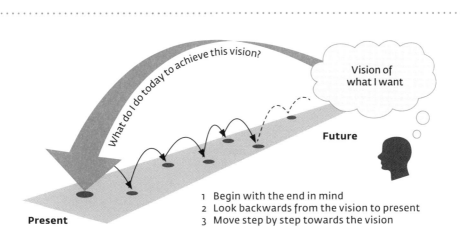

1 Begin with the end in mind
2 Look backwards from the vision to present
3 Move step by step towards the vision

The sustainability strategy focuses on creating sustainable value. There is an increasing number of articles and books that explain what sustainable value creation is or should be, using terms such as multiple value creation, shared value, WEconomy, the UN Global Compact's Post-2015 Business Engagement Architecture or the Doughnut Economy (Figure 3.1). These are new models and frameworks for business and market mechanisms, which necessitate a fundamental change from the business sector. Such changes require a clear strategy, one that makes the steps towards sustainable value creation concrete. An example of this is a case study published by The Natural Step[3], as shown in Figure 3.2. The building blocks of the framework for strategic sustainable development — highlighted in the case study — might also inspire companies: whole systems thinking, four science-based sustainability principles and back-casting. Back-casting is a type of creative thinking that starts from the desired end result, asks how it is possible to get there and translates this into an action plan.

Despite all these great theories and scientific frameworks, a practical way of creating, "a sustainable value strategy", is to combine societal needs and your stakeholder interests with the core business and resources of your company, guided by the moral compass of your mission or purpose. The latter is important because the strategy should not only be about seizing market opportunities — while adding value for society at the same time — but should really build on your envisaged role in (and contribution to) society.

A company has a wide range of means to create sustainable value and thus contribute to society. It has the economic power to produce new sustainable products and services; it also has the political power to rewrite the rules of the game by developing new codes of conduct or new sustainable business models. Business assets such as buildings, sites, materials, networks, financial and intellectual resources, employees or even its media range or customers can be used to create sustainable value, which is shown in the paragraph about the successful Strategist in this chapter.

Transition

For existing companies, transformation processes and systems change often take years. There are various models that describe the different steps a company goes through in the transitions towards sustainable value creation. In the article, "Chief Sustainability Officers: Who Are They and What Do They Do?" Kathleen Miller and George Serafeim explore the ways in which firms (CSOs) move sustainability into the core of the organization. Based on their research, they define three stages of the degree to which sustainability has become a core concern of the organization: from the "compliance" stage, and the "efficiency" stage to the most advanced stage of development, the "innovation" stage. These type of maturity models are well suited to track — and steer — the change process. Two other examples are the Maturity Model by Rob van Tilburg and Rob van Tulder[4] and the Gearing Up Framework by Avastone Consulting.[5] The latter maps the transition process as well as the various tipping points and success factors within it. It is outlined in more detail in Chapter 4 on the Coordinator role of the sustainability manager, as tracking and steering the transition process is part of that role.

Both models provide their own interpretation of the strategic focus of companies at the most developed phase of sustainable business or sustainable value creation. In Van Tilburg's and Van Tulder's model, the most developed phase is the proactive phase, in which the company actively displays leadership on large social issues. Within companies in that phase, the strategic focus reaches far beyond the societal developments that directly impact the individual company. Instead, they (also) consider what is relevant for society at large. In Avastone's Framework, the highest gear in sustainable value creation is redesign, a phase in which companies contribute to systemic change by banishing the causes of non-sustainability.

Signaling trends

Within most companies, the strategy department or team is in charge of the process to create the vision and mission. This process is fueled by external trends and developments, both those that influence the company and those on which the company has (or wants to have) an influence.

Within the strategy process, the sustainability manager should provide relevant trends and topics, including the (future) material topics of the stakeholders. It is important to be explicit when asking stakeholders what they see as future topics, as they are what determine the relevant sustainable value the company can create for them. Another source of relevant information is annual reports of similar companies.

To provide general societal trends, you can make use of trend reports, such as those created by the World Business Council for Sustainable Development or local CSR organizations. The most relevant global sustainability topics are brought together in the UN Sustainable Development Goals (Figure 3.3). There are seventeen goals, of which a selection can be relevant in the context of the current and future activities of your company: either as an opportunity or as a risk as well as eliminating the negative impact a company might have on the "remaining" goals. A clearer path forward for companies is provided by the World Benchmarking Alliance (WBA). It has identified seven vital systems transformations to accomplish the 2030 Agenda and listed the industries that are particularly important for driving each transformation. In addition, GRI, the UN Global Compact and the World Business Council for Sustainable Development (WBCSD) have developed "The SDG Compass"[6], which provides guidance for companies on how they can align their strategies as well as measure and manage their contribution towards the realization of SDGs.

FIGURE 3.3 **UN Sustainable Development Goals**

Integrated vision

When your company has already developed a vision and mission, you can work with the strategy department to review it and to make it relevant to society. You can do this by exploring how society is changing and how the company can connect its core activities to a societal role in these changes. Examples of this: "healthy aging" for pension funds and "connecting people" for airlines.

Ideally, the company vision and mission are aligned with the sustainability vision and mission, as is the case with Patagonia "We're in business to save our home planet" or Unilever "to make sustainable living commonplace" or DSM "our purpose is to create brighter lives for all". With such an integrated vision or corporate purpose, it is easier to integrate sustainability into the corporate strategy and activities than when a separate, sustainability vision and mission are developed.

Marco Krapels (CEO Micropower, former VP Tesla, former Executive VP Rabobank NA and co-chair of the Rabobank's CSR committee):

> *"The success of Tesla is that they aim to create a sustainable lifestyle with no compromise. Every innovation or business should be the best, sexiest, most attractive product for the consumer. Sustainability is therefore a key condition — that the product itself contributes to the mission — rather than just a driver for innovation."*

Developing a vision

During the development of a separated (specific) vision and mission for sustainability, the role of the sustainability manager goes beyond providing relevant sustainability topics and context. In that case, the sustainability manager is in charge of the process. During the creation process, this is key to developing support, both with external stakeholders and senior management. This requires an intensive effort, a process during which the sustainability manager is not just the Strategist, but also needs to activate the Networker and the Connector roles to generate external and internal support for the vision. As CSO or CSR manager, do consider whether it is worth the effort. It is worth it when senior management has come up with an inspiring sustainability vision and mission and is willing to translate this into a sustainability strategy with concrete goals that can be externally communicated.

If you expect that a separated vision and mission will end up shelved in a filing cabinet, together with other projects for which the time has not yet come, then perhaps it is better to wait or to be very pragmatic about it.

"Go with the flow, work with those people within the organization who are eager to contribute. Direct your energy where it is already flowing. Make those things better and larger and do not waste too much energy on convincing people resisting the integration of sustainability in the company's strategy."

ELFRIEKE VAN GALEN (CO-FOUNDER SUSTAINABILITY UNIVERSITY FOUNDATION)

A practical way to derive a separated vision is to map what sustainability activities are already taking place within the company. You then set a realistic yet ambitious sustainability goal, both in increasing your positive activities and in reducing your negative impact, such as CO_2 emissions. In addition, it is effective to link these sustainability goals to the core activity of a company. For an energy-intensive company, examples could be "10% energy reduction within five years" or "convert to renewable energy".

Motivated intrinsically or by the business case?

When creating a vision and mission, the matter of "why?" or corporate purpose quickly comes up. To answer the why-question, you can use Simon Sinek's golden circle, as shown in Figure 3.4. Sinek states that most companies know *what* they do, many companies know *how* they do it, yet only a few companies know *why* they do it or, in other words, what added value they provide to society. He then states that those companies that know very well why they exist are the ones that inspire and attract clients and talent. He advises companies to think from the inside out and start with why.

FIGURE 3.4 **Simon Sinek's Golden Circle**

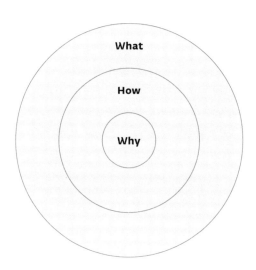

You can also apply the Sinek way of thinking to your sustainability vision and mission or corporate purpose. As an organization, do you want to become more sustainable because you can make more money that way or because you can improve the world? Or both? Is it even possible to do both? And if a more sustainable world is your goal, how do you achieve that? The answers to these questions can basically be divided into two categories: the intrinsically motivated and the business-case driven. This is not just a case of semantics, these can really feel like opposing camps. When working on the why-question, a moral discussion often arises as to whether a company is "really" sustainable if its considerations for sustainable business are more commercial or businesslike.

There is a strong conviction (and some scientific evidence[7]) that companies that are intrinsically motivated for sustainable business are more effective than those which are not. The underlying assumption is that employees will commit much earlier and longer to an intrinsically motivated vision of "doing the right thing". Another conviction is that the company that wants to create economic value with sustainable business will be more effective. Companies have a strong impulse to anchor sustainable business if they are looking for ways to make money by solving societal issues. After all, most companies are equipped to make money and are familiar with thinking in business cases. So, when more money can be made (or when other economic value can be created, like an enhanced reputation) through more sustainable business practices, this fits well within existing structures and methods. You may actually not have to choose. It is a great proposition to have a strong business case, also when you are intrinsically motivated. In addition, a sustainability strategy initially based on a business case or extrinsic factors can lead to intrinsic motivation or vice versa.

"We are driven by the legacy that we want to leave. The change of business automatically changed the focus of our sustainability activities in addressing energy challenges, to ensure a power supply that is reliable and sustainable. We operate from a value-based perspective: buying more clean energy, especially near our operations, helps us operate more sustainably and makes good business sense."

BRIAN JANOUS (GENERAL MANAGER OF ENERGY AND SUSTAINABILITY AT MICROSOFT)

Value drivers of sustainable business

The overview of the Sustainable Value Framework by Stuart L. Hart and Mark B. Milstein can help to develop and substantiate a strategy. The framework, as shown in Figure 3.5, shows relevant business perspectives (risk reduction, cost reduction, innovation and commercial success, reputation and growth) that can support both a more sustainable world and shareholder value in parallel. From whatever perspective or motivation, the sustainability strategy shows a clear win-win in each quadrant.

The quadrants of Figure 3.5 can be used to build a business case: along one axis ranging from improving current activities to the development of new technologies and markets in the future and a second axis ranging from using internal possibilities to external engagement. There are four core dimensions of a sustainability strategy with different links to company performance and value creation for stakeholders:

- Growing profits and reducing risks through preventing waste in the current operation (for example eco-efficiency measures)
- Enhancing reputation and legitimacy through stakeholder engagement and product life cycle improvements (sustainable business and product stewardship)
- Accelerating innovation and repositioning through the development and use of next generation sustainable technologies (clean technologies)
- Crystallizing the firm's growth path and trajectory through co-creation of new activities, focused on serving the needs of those most needy in society (base of the pyramid).

Ideally, according to Hart, companies operate in all four quadrants supporting a more holistic approach: but you do not have to. It is a choice, that, of course, does impact the further integration of sustainability into the overall

FIGURE 3.5 **Sustainable Value Framework** (inspired by Stuart L. Hart and Mark B. Milstein)

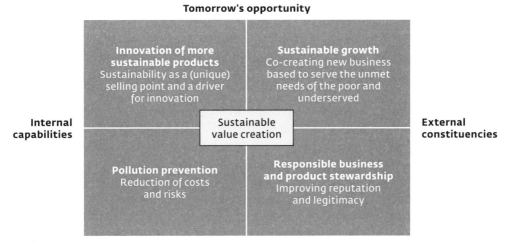

corporate strategy. Connecting sustainability to repositioning and company growth seems to lead to a more integrated sustainability strategy, rather than connecting it merely to cost and risk reduction by limiting the environmental footprint. There is a certain similarity between the upper right-hand quadrant of Hart and Milstein's framework and the most developed phase of a corporate sustainability maturity model. This is because, in the most mature phase, the company is intrinsically motivated to search for a strategy that delivers (sustainable) value for society.

It is important for sustainability managers to realize that, to act more sustainably, companies and people can be motivated by different reasons.

"Sustainability is driven by both a business case and for good stewardship. With Kellogg, it started as a corporate and founder value and evolved into a business strategy. For a global consumer brand, it is essential to rely on a sustainable food system."

DIANE HOLDORF (MANAGING DIRECTOR FOOD & NATURE, WORLD BUSINESS COUNCIL FOR SUSTAINABLE DEVELOPMENT, FORMER CSO AND VP OF ENVIRONMENTAL STEWARDSHIP, HEALTH AND SAFETY OF KELLOGG COMPANY)

3.2 Sustainable value creation in practice

The models mentioned in this chapter provide insight and overview. They help to identify the elements of a solid business case for sustainability. At NS, elements of the business case are cost reduction by energy and waste reduction programs, increased customer loyalty because they like to travel without CO_2 emissions, and more motivated employees who are happy to share the sustainability credentials. Finally, new markets for sustainable mobility are developed in collaboration with partners, replacing less sustainable modes of transport. This again leads to a reduction in CO_2 and particulate matter emissions. The value of many of these elements can be mapped with the help of research and output data, including the less tangible, such as a better reputation.

The primary business drivers for sustainability often relate to the level of maturity of sustainability in a business. Michael Kobori (former VP Sustainability at Levi Strauss & Co.) distinguishes three groups of business benefits — in order of level of maturity of sustainability in a business (from low to high):

1 Risk management and reputation:
   a avoiding negative media coverage or negative feedback from stakeholders
   b actual operational risks (extreme weather effects due to climate change can disrupt deliveries).

2 Productivity issues:
   a less water and energy (save money)
   b renewables (save money)
   c attracting and retaining talent.
3 Contribute to growth:
   a constant innovation (e.g. laser repair of authentic vintage Levi's)
   b building of brand — next generation of consumers — born after 1995
      (like Greta Thunberg).

As a consequence, in general, one can also measure level of maturity of sustainability by involvement of different departments during the years (from low to high):
1 Legal department: regulatory compliance
2 Communication team: reputation management
3 Supply chain team: cost and delivery disruption
4 Finance team: productivity and investments
5 Brand team and marketing: brand equity
6 Commercial sales: customer engagement and growth
7 Board and shareholders: future resilience.

Creating a "why"

In March 2010, the first program for sustainable business was reviewed and approved for a three-year term by the board. The vision and mission were stated as follows: "NS takes leadership in the area of sustainability from a conviction that this is the basis for continuity and profitability as well as from an obligation towards our clients, society and our employees."

The 2010 vision and mission show an intrinsic as well as an extrinsic motivation, but at that point in time, the *why* behind the intrinsic conviction was not discussed. This conversation came two years later when it became clear that the lack of this *why* was making it difficult to clearly tell the story behind this conviction. To guide this discussion in a strategic way, Simon Sinek's golden circle (Figure 3.4) was really useful.

NS started crafting the story of its *why* by engaging its top management layer (thirty-five people). The process started by asking everyone to define their personal *why* and to then define the NS-why from that angle. The *why* probably has to be updated over time; for example, after changes in the board, but the initial *why*, "together contributing to progress by bringing people to people in a sustainable way", could still be very valid to date.

Every year, management signs off on the sustainability program. The new plan is framed in light of the vision and mission. In parallel, achievements are presented within the context of the business case as well as the activities planned to achieve our mission, and an update on the anchoring of sustainability in the organization.

Integrated vision in practice

One of the companies known for its successful integrated vision is Unilever. Its vision and mission is to make sustainable living commonplace. In 2010, the company launched the Unilever Sustainable Living Plan, which basically aims at sustainable growth: growing the size of the company and at the same time halving the environmental impact or footprint of the products by 2030. In addition, they also want to improve the health and well-being of more than one billion (!) people and improve the standard of living of the millions of people who work in Unilever's total value chain, both by 2020.

"In the process of developing the Unilever Sustainable Living Plan, it was very important that we had the courage to be bold. It was essential to put big audacious goals out there which we were convinced it is the right direction and we should be aiming for, even if we didn't yet have all the answers on just how to get there. Being ambitious results in a certain internal discomfort, which is key to getting things moving. Settling for goals, which you know (you) will reach if you just follow the roadmap and subsequently lying back and taking it easy, is a trap. This is a luxury we cannot afford. The agenda for the world, laid down in the SDGs, is simply too urgent."

Thus spoke Anniek Mauser, sustainability director Benelux at Unilever, who was part of the team working on developing the Unilever Sustainable Living Plan at that time.

Part of the process is annual reporting on the progress. The annual progress reports still contain positive messages. In its own words, the Unilever report mid-2018:

"We're eight years into our ten-year plan and we've learnt a huge amount. We know the transformational change we want to see within our business and beyond will take more than 'business as usual' solutions. New technologies, new business models, new ways of thinking and new collaborations — they are all vital to creating the inclusive growth that will ensure a sustainable future for the world, its people and our business."

3.3   The learning Strategist

A dynamic business case and pragmatic approach

From the start, NS chose a two-pronged approach: an intrinsic conviction joined with an economic business case for sustainable business. This approach generated sufficient support as it appealed to many different people. To communicate the integrated strategy, a cube with visuals of the six strategic themes was used (Figure 3.6). We learned that this cube was very useful to explain the sustainable strategy and how sustainability was related to the core activities and strategic themes.

FIGURE 3.6 **Strategic cube**

In parallel, a more qualitative business case for sustainable business was presented, highlighting the benefits for the company and for society in terms of CO_2 reduction and euros. The business case was updated yearly and Table 3.1 shows how some of the elements of the business case gained or lost

TABLE 3.1 **Development of the core elements in the case for sustainable business**

Consistently important	Increased in importance	Decreased in importance
Our customers want sustainable mobility Maintain top line (market share)	Reputation, positive media attention Opportunity for top line growth	Labor market communications
Employees: connection, pride, and innovative drivers	Clients and customers: environment becoming increasingly important for those travelers that have a choice between car and train	
Cost reduction	Collaboration with partners Social value	

importance over time. The core of the business case — this is what customers and clients want — increased in importance over time.

The qualitative business case strengthened over time, supported by metrics such as the change in use of public transport and cost savings. The business case also progressed with the development of the corporate strategy, in which reputation became increasingly important.

Be alert to a change of board or CEO

A change of board or CEO is always a moment of recalibration of the business strategy. And, therefore, as I have learned myself but also hear from other CSOs, a moment to be extra alert. In the eight years that I was active as a CSO at NS, a change of board happened twice. The first time it happened, sustainability was removed from the list of six strategic spearheads and thus not explicitly mentioned in the strategy (anymore). The expectation of the new CEO was that sustainability was sufficiently anchored in the DNA of the organization, vision and ambition. Also, the number of strategic themes needed to be limited in order to focus more on improving operational performance. The line of reasoning makes sense, because good operational performance is a condition for sustainable growth. However, the removal of sustainability as one of the strategic themes had consequences; it started to lead a life of its own. A quote from the summary of an internal advisory report on the positioning of sustainability within NS, gives immediate insight into these consequences: "Sustainability is dealt with in various ways in available strategic documents, the annual report, target letters and other means of control, so that the meaning, status and position of sustainability is unclear". This lack of clarity was caused by the fact that sustainability was first a strategic spearhead and then shifted to part of the ambition, without turning that shift into a specific point of attention. The result was that each department made an individual choice or estimate about how much attention was to be given to making the company more sustainable. That resulted in major differences between the departments: a clear signal for me to be on board for the second reviewing of the business strategy. I made a great effort to be invited and to become part of the strategy process, since a CSO (like me) is often seen as a program manager with a Coordinating role and not as someone with a Strategic role. However, the *sustainer* wins: the new ambitious 2025 strategy clearly mentions "always sustainable!"

3.4 The successful Strategist

Business/corporations are extremely important when it comes to accelerating transitions. A successful Strategist navigates his or her business towards the creating of sustainable value for the company and for society. Marco Krapels's (CEO Micropower, former VP Tesla) "boost the energy transition" story started when he became co-chair of the Rabobank's Corporate Social Responsibility committee. At that time, he was Executive Vice President of Rabobank, N.A. (part of the Rabobank Group), a California-based community bank, providing personalized service and a full array of quality products through local decision-making and active community involvement.

Marco Krapels explains:

"With the housing of ninety-one retail branches and fifteen financial service centers from Sacramento to the Imperial Valley, we owned assets that we could use to boost the energy transition. We decided to install solar at as many locations as possible, to offset electricity used by the location and, in addition, to provide renewable energy to charge electric cars of customers, local shoppers and employees. This was a good business decision because solar power makes economic sense. It allowed us to get a long-term fixed energy price in a volatile market where energy prices were forecasted to spike, especially during peak hours. In addition, it showed that we cared about our community, and therefore supported our reputation and customer relations."

"In 2009 we decided to take the renewable energy movement to a next level and created the world's first solar-power enhanced, fast-charge electric car charging corridor, together with SolarCity® (a company co-founded by Elon Musk) and Tesla Motors. The corridor between San Francisco and Los Angeles includes four bank branch locations and a fifth in a public parking garage, allowing all-electric cars to make the trip using solar energy and provide for the fastest charge time available for public electric vehicle (EV) charges. The corridor was the first interregional effort of its kind and the first to include solar power at a charging station. The bank branches of the Rabobank were very important in the transition to EV because they allowed EV drivers to take longer trips and so use the EV as their primary car."

This best practice shows the role of companies and business in accelerating the (energy) transition to a sustainable world. Companies can use their assets in a way that makes economic sense and contributes to a sustainable world. It is the Strategic role of a Corporate Social Responsibility committee or Corporate Sustainability Officer to seize these sustainable business opportunities.

Marco Krapels:

> *"Big energy consumers like Microsoft, Google (datacenters), NS (trains) and Unilever lead by example through their innovative and economically sound renewables policy. Big companies can be the frontrunners of transitions, and as soon as other companies and even energy directors see it as sound economic policy, it will be an unstoppable trend. It already is, we are beyond the point of no return!"*

Renewable energy — wind for the trains — Strategic role

The first sustainable business program of NS started with activities focused on reducing negative environmental impact such as greenhouse gas emissions, waste, and noise. It also stated an intent to engage with various stakeholders to discuss the focus areas in the future, but to first start with a baseline measurement (part of the Monitor role). Lastly, the program included a plan to create more cohesion, to focus on the many CSR activities already in place and the ambition — as a responsible employer — to include our social activities in our sustainability report. In short, the strategy was all about "measurement for knowledge". As CSO, the main focus of my Strategic role was closely related to (or "substituted" by) the tasks of the Monitor and Coordinator roles.

After a few years of building credibility and trust with the board by showing results, progress and facts, I felt it was time to step up in my Strategic role. The train could lose its leading position in sustainable mobility to the car industry. The car industry was innovating much faster than the train industry and investing substantially in sustainable technologies and marketing. In addition, because of our small leverage (buying power), it would be difficult to stimulate the train industry to speed up its innovations.

I created a sense of urgency with the board by showing them a simple graph, indicating the curve of the well to wheel CO_2 emission of cars versus our trains over time, as is shown in Figure 3.7. This graph made it clear that we had to act immediately in order to keep our leading position and license to grow.

FIGURE 3.7 **Well to wheel CO₂ emissions of cars versus trains over time**

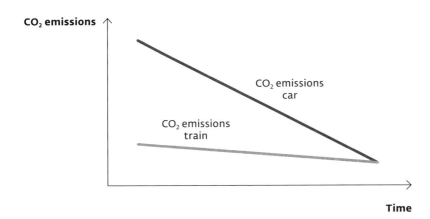

The sense of urgency that I created in my Strategic role, was the starting point to search for 100% renewables for the trains. Only by running on renewables, could trains stay ahead of the competition and continue to offer the most sustainable mode of long-distance travel.

Tips for Strategists

- Adjust your strategy role to the space you are granted within the organization.
- Develop a sustainability vision and mission aligned with the corporate vision and mission. Find intrinsic convictions by discussing the "why" behind it. Start crafting the story of the corporate purpose together with senior management.
- Look at the current corporate vision and mission through a sustainability lens and add societal topics.
- When looking through the sustainability lens at changes in society, explicitly highlight positive developments and subsequently assess the risks and opportunities they present. Create a sense of urgency.
- In case you are starting a separate strategy process, make use of existing methods in the company, collaborate with the teams and departments in charge of such processes. This, for example, could take you outside your own office, to international headquarters.
- Do not get distracted by the different expectations about what the vision of the company should be. In the end, it is all about how you positively impact society as a company and how effectively you direct these efforts.
- A change in vision and mission is a matter of timing and being sensitive to what the company wants and can handle. Be bold and ambitious if you can.
- Choose a more practical approach if the organization is not ready yet for an ambitious vision. Be pragmatic in building a business case using the information that you have.
- Increase the level of maturity of sustainability — and related sustainable strategy — by building on various business drivers for sustainability. Always connect sustainability to the core business of the company to prevent it from becoming a peripheral, non-strategic activity.
- Ensure you are at the table when a strategy revision process kicks off. Be alert with a change of board or CEO.
- Engage other people in the development of your vision and mission; for example, people from sales, other regions or people with a completely different view. This generates support and creativity. Give them feedback on what will be done with their input.
- Where considering the creation of a separate sustainability vision and mission, weigh the costs in hours and energy against the expected benefits. How will the organization act on it in the end?
- Use your company's assets in a way that that makes economic sense and contributes to a sustainable world. A successful Strategist should seize these sustainable business opportunities.

4

The Coordinator & Initiator

"The gardener does not make a plant grow. The job of the gardener is to create optimal conditions."

SIR KEN ROBINSON, WRITER, EMERITUS PROFESSOR, AND EDUCATION EXPERT

An important task of the CSO is to support the organization and its different departments by initiating and embedding sustainability in the governance and organizational structure of an organization. This is the Coordinator & Initiator role. You are aware of the changes sparked by the sustainability strategy. You organize, coordinate and facilitate departments, people, processes, change and projects to deliver on the strategy using the governance and organizational management structure. However, the true responsibility for implementation and achievement of the sustainability goals is with those department and people themselves. The CSO or CSR manager supports and coaches when the performance and the anchoring of the sustainability strategy lag behind.

In the Coordinator & Initiator role, the CSO needs a deep understanding of how the company is organized and governed to be able to anchor sustainability in the structure, systems and processes. It is important to visualize, understand and analyze how the company works. Only with insight into the company's core processes and the cohesion across them, can you optimally translate and adjust the (integrated) CSR strategy for the organization. In addition, you need to be aware of systems inside and outside the organization, such as the supply chain. And you need to be aware what needs to happen to change these systems.

"Linking sustainability to your brand strategy will lead to the sustainability agenda becoming one with the business agenda. This will anchor ownership and drive for sustainability in the organization and accelerate progress."

ESTHER VERBURG — VICE-PRESIDENT OF CORPORATE RESPONSIBILITY
AT TOMMY HILFIGER GLOBAL/PVH EUROPE

This chapter highlights the tasks related to translating the vision, mission and strategy into the organization. It will include working with others to create an integrated plan or strategic framework, which supports relevant departments in developing their own plans to achieve the sustainability goals. In addition, it covers how to structure the sustainability efforts to best support the company and it provides examples of initiatives undertaken to achieve sustainable change in a company's system. Initially, to set things in motion, this might include starting (iconic) projects yourself.

4.1 The strategic framework or sustainability plan

To turn the vision, mission and strategy into action, most companies create a strategic framework. Such a framework guides the different plans within the organization. The sum of these plans and their implementation should ensure that the ambition and strategy are fulfilled. When sustainability is integrated into the overall corporate strategy, then the translation of strategy into action for sustainability will also align with the regular strategic planning process, including being an integral part of the strategic framework.

Framework elements

The strategic framework or sustainability plan usually includes:

- The key topics or areas on which progress is needed
- The principles or frames based upon which action will be taken
- The key performance indicators used to measure results
- The baseline/starting point and the goals to be achieved.

Based on these elements of the strategic framework, departments and teams within the organization can create their own plans to achieve the goals, using measures, activities and projects.

The CSO or CSR manager will adjust the level of detail and concretization of the strategic framework so that it will fit into the "regular" strategic planning process, fitting the way the company is organized.

In a highly decentralized organization, the strategic framework will be much less detailed than in a centrally led organization. In that case, the Coordinator role of the CSO or CSR manager will be less content-driven and more process-driven: a process to engage senior management to set concrete targets and work with them to develop plans. Engaging them also generates support for the implementation.

To further increase supportive action, it is important to translate the strategic framework and the goals into other governmental elements like job descriptions and appraisal processes. Sustainability performance can become part of the remuneration system for senior management and others in the organization. This is a clear way for a company to raise awareness about its commitment to sustainability and fuel its transition process to a sustainable organization. Translation should therefore cover all business processes, including supportive business processes. Chapter 6 on the Mentor role describes the way in which you can involve all business processes and jointly define the sustainable actions as well as "sub indicators" for each business process. How to define indicators and metrics are part of the Monitor role (Chapter 8).

It takes quite some coordinating power to safeguard that the sum of all derived plans add up to the intended strategy and results, focused on the key topics. This is part of the Coordinator role of the CSO or CSR manager or, in

TABLE 4.1 **Examples of key elements of NS's strategic framework**

Description	Examples
Topics	Energy, waste, sustainable image/brand
Principles	• Focus on the source: reduction, reuse (waste) or renewable (energy) • Procurement of renewable energy: additional and traceable sources • Avoid CO_2 compensation
Key performance indicators	• Energy use and CO_2 emissions per traveled kilometer • Weight of waste streams • Ranking in list of most sustainable companies in the Netherlands
Targets for 2020	• Energy is 50% more efficient than in 2005 • No more CO_2 emissions for energy use • 75% reuse of materials • 25% reduction in weight streams compared to 2014 • Top ten ranking most sustainable companies in the Netherlands

the case that sustainability is well integrated, for senior management or the director of strategy. Table 4.1 contains examples from NS's strategic framework for sustainability.

Clear starting points

When the vision, mission, strategy and framework are very clear, the translation of sustainability to the organization can focus on how each employee can contribute to the mission personally, within his/her own role. As the term sustainability means different things to different people, it is key to make the framework as clear as possible with clarity regarding priorities and choices made. Former sustainability director Steve Howard of IKEA, highlighted the importance of clear goals in a TED Talk:

> *"A target of 100% is easier to achieve than one of 90%, as most people will assume that they belong to the 10% that does not have to achieve the goal."*

Since a 100% target is not always achievable in practice, effective target setting requires being clear on the exceptions.

With clear starting points, the Coordinator role can be mostly directed at supporting the business in achieving their goals and coaching, when performance lags behind. In Chapter 3, on the Strategic role, I described the example of the integrated vision of Unilever, "to make sustainable living commonplace," and its big audacious strategic goal. In addition, the company has developed the Unilever Sustainable Living Plan, a detailed blueprint covering all aspects of its global business and value chain, so that the business knows what starting points to use to achieve sustainable growth, or as Anniek Mauser puts it, "to get things moving".

The Coordinator role of the CSO or CSR manager will take more time in the case that sustainability is not integrated into corporate strategy. Even in that scenario, it is best to have the derived sustainability strategy align as much as possible with the existing processes for strategic planning and implementation. Using the same language (formats and expressions) will facilitate the integration and embedding of sustainability into the organization's activities.

Embedding sustainability

Knowledge of change management can be valuable for CSR or sustainability managers, especially in the Coordinator role. Partly inspired by John Kotter's change theory, the following five S's can be used to embed sustainability in the organization:

1 Stakeholders
2 Strategy (leadership)
3 Support (values)
4 Structures
5 Systems.

Stakeholders and strategy have been covered in Chapters 2 and 3. Support is all about the internal backing and the softer elements of change, such as shared values. This will be covered in Chapters 5 and 6. This chapter and Chapter 8 focus on using structures and systems to anchor sustainability in the organization. Structure relates to the way in which the company is organized and governed. In most companies, the strategic framework plays a key role in this. System relates to the way in which the company is supported; for example, through processes and technologies to deliver products and services. Chapter 8 covers the Monitor role of the CSO or CSR manager, including the process to determine the performance indicators, base line measurements and metrics. It also covers adjustment and continuous improvement, as the final elements of the overall performance cycle.

Changing organizations

To align itself well with its changing context, an organization will evolve continuously, as will the five S's around it. As Coordinator, be aware of changes, such as a change in the company's structure. For example, when a company changes from production-driven to process-driven, it is important to take the embedding of sustainability into account in this change. In that case, the people responsible for key processes in a company should also be made responsible for the sustainability of these processes.

Initiating activities

As the ultimate responsibility for the implementation of the sustainability strategy is with the departments and people themselves, as Coordinator you are dependent on their appetite for change and their implementation speed. Things can take longer than desired, which is especially challenging when trying to demonstrate progress to stakeholders. As the CSO or CSR manager, you can then initiate or accelerate change by carrying out select sustainability projects or initiatives yourself or with the support of a (temporary) small-scale project management office.

Initiating projects or activities yourself, with the aim of having the current organization take them over later, can be especially useful when:

- There is a lack of capacity, capability or priority in the current organization. In the case of stepping in yourself to create extra capacity, do make clear agreements for a later transfer of ownership.
- The focus is on new sustainability topics. For example, in the area of reporting, the sustainability team might initially lead the development of an environmental profit & loss account (instead of finance).
- There is a need for an appealing iconic project to show how sustainability leads to success.

These so-called pilots or temporary activities, when proven successful, are rolled out and owned by other parts of the organizations. This can be very quick or take years, depending on the project's complexity and the willingness of the existing organization to take on the activity or project. It is a golden rule among sustainability professionals that, if you cannot find a business owner within three years for a project that you initiated, you should stop the project.

By carrying out projects yourself you do not just initiate change, your project also offers opportunities to strengthen your internal networks; for example, by working together with departments, such as the facilities team, which are important for making the internal organization more sustainable.

4.2 Making plans, implementing and embedding in practice

All departments at NS generate action plans based on a strategic framework, in which sustainability is integrated. This strategic framework is signed off by the management board. With the update of the framework, the sustainability plan needs an update as well. As the CSO, I ensured that the sustainability plan had sufficient support from those managers required to take the sustainability plan deeper into the organization.

Establishing goals

Throughout the years, the sustainability goals became increasingly concrete or larger in scale: each topic at its own speed. For example, the waste management strategy is to have waste serve as a raw material for new products and the goals to help achieve this become more concrete each year. This is due to:

- Improved insight into different waste streams over time
- The growing availability of solutions that could help achieve the goals
- An increase in the number of partners willing to contribute to solutions
- Difference in local color, even in a country as small as the Netherlands.

Good target setting is a very important process if you want to create sustainable success. Most companies adhere to the safe management rule of, "underpromise and overdeliver". However, that will not get you the best solutions and change that is needed.

Neil Hawkins (former Corporate Vice President and Chief Sustainability Officer of Dow Inc.) agrees that good target setting is key to moving forward: "It has to be a realistic stretch. Enough challenge and realistic at the same time, with an inspiring vision about a flourishing world: let's do/make this together. It is very important to set long range ambitious goals because big problems ask for big goals and goals that need system change cannot be reached by incremental change. In addition, the magic comes in the goal-setting process, when you set a goal that is possible to reach only when there is coordination between the business units."

The dynamics of Dow's goal-setting over the years can best be explained by Footprint, Handprint and then Blueprint:
- Footprint: in 1995 -2005 — the first goals were set on energy and safety to prove the point that sustainability adds to the triple bottom line: good for the environment, social and also for economics
- Handprint: then another set of ten years 2005-2015 goals were set on the products
- Blueprint: and the latest set of goals 2015-2025 were goals to lead and solve public problems (for example, watershed management).

In 1992, an external Advisory Council with leaders from NGOs, government, the academic world and business, was started by Dow in order to set these goals and to challenge the company. This Council still has semi-annual three-day meetings with the board to discuss what the world will look like in 2097 and what Dow's position should be in that world. And derived from that — what Dow's position should then be in ten years. In addition, community Advisory Panels at sites/locations were installed to align the rest of the organization.

Neil Hawkins:

"A CSO should change an 'underpromise and overdeliver culture', into a 'smart risk-taking culture' when it comes to sustainability. If you set 90% target and you make it 84% then maybe you have failed, but you also know that without setting the 90% you would have never come as far as 84%. The golden rule of underpromise and overdeliver should be used for sales/ revenues/safety and so on, but not for sustainability."

Identifying opportunities

Any changes in an organization pose potential risks for the sustainability focus. For example, when NS updated its strategy, sustainability seemed to have disappeared from the priorities. It was well integrated into the vision and ambition, but was no longer explicitly mentioned as a pillar in the strategy. Internally, this was perceived as a signal that senior management had placed sustainability lower on its list of priorities. To overcome this perception issue, the Coordinator role of the CSR manager increased significantly. It required a serious communication effort to explain that sustainability continued to be important and to ensure that the sustainability goals were still met.

Changes can also pose opportunities. A change to a more process-oriented structure, for example, makes it easier to integrate sustainability into topics like waste management. Typically, waste management involves different business processes, such as procurement, facility management, operations, logistics and maintenance, from "entering the company to reuse after leaving the company". It is effective to have one manager to take responsibility for the entire waste flow. Obviously, this role should be agreed upon with the managers of all relevant business processes and, in a more process-oriented structure, this is more likely to be accepted. In your Coordinator role, you can assess, for each sustainability topic, whether such a process structure is needed and feasible.

Each change provides opportunities to bring sustainability into the conversation and to assess how it can best be integrated into the organization. Each introductory meeting with a new colleague is an opportunity to find a new sustainability ambassador. The more change there is, the faster sustainability can be integrated into the organization. But it does require the CSR manager to actively seek opportunities. As Winston Churchill said:

> *"The pessimist sees problems in every opportunity.*
> *The optimist sees opportunities in each problem."*

Structuring the sustainability team

The structure and size of the sustainability team need to be in line with what is required to further the integration of sustainability into the business. This all depends on how the company is structured and to the degree to which sustainability is embedded already. There are three phases to integrating sustainability often referred to as: initiation, development and maintenance. These phases go hand in hand with the levels of maturity mentioned earlier in Chapter 3 on the Strategic role: compliance, efficiency and innovation.

Initiation phase is related to the level at which a company has the basics of CSR or Sustainability program in place; for example, on a project basis. Development phase is related to the level that a company is (beginning or well) on its way towards fully embedding sustainability. The maintenance phase is related to the level at which CSR is fully embedded within the organization and the company is an industry game changer through sustainability.

During the initiation and early development phases, the time spent by the sustainability team on generic embedding activities increases until the later development phase. In the initiation phase, the sustainability team is usually also quite small. The CSO role might even be a part-time role, mostly focused on mapping and stimulating existing initiatives in the company and starting up a few new initiatives. In the development phase, the sustainability team's efforts become more specific since it is clearer what the organization needs. During that phase, knowledge and innovations are developed and transferred to the existing organization. In the maintenance phase, most of the sustainability efforts are led and implemented by the existing organization. Often the location of the CSO in the organization moves to where it adds the most value. As the maturity level grows, frequently the authority of the CSO also grows, even in the more mature phases, when sustainability is embedded and responsibilities of the CSO will change.

The structure, efforts and location of the sustainability team in the organization also need to be aligned with the way in which change is managed at the operational level. This differs widely in each organization and therefore requires the CSR manager to create tailor-made solutions, based on in-depth knowledge of the organization.

"Tesla's mission is to accelerate the world's transition to sustainable energy. Elon Musk (CEO) is the most mission-driven leader that I know. If you work for/with him, he tells you: 'You do not have a job, you have a mission.' To work with Elon is very inspiring. Tesla is a very flat organization. There is no Corporate Sustainability Officer because every person who works at Tesla has to incorporate and live the mission."

MARCO KRAPELS (CEO MICROPOWER, FORMER VP TESLA, EXECUTIVE VP RABOBANK, N.A. AND CO-CHAIR OF THE RABOBANK'S CSR COMMITTEE)

The structure and size of the sustainability team also depend on the portfolio of sustainability activities for which the team is responsible. Harvard

67

research[8] shows that sustainability initiatives are usually quite spread out and uncoordinated across the company. In such a case, more value can be created by better coordination across various initiatives focused on charity, efficiency and new business models. This is also discussed in paragraph 5.4 about foundations.

The sustainability organization at NS

At NS, I have always used existing organizational processes, systems and structures to organize sustainability. This makes it easier to embed sustainability activities. NS consists of a few business units and a small holding company. The organization is led by the management board. Should this structure change, the organization of the sustainability team would potentially change as well.

When setting up the sustainability team, I explored how other large organizations did this, what was successful and what could be reapplied at NS. The sustainability structure at NS is a functional matrix organization with a small, temporary staff team, a working group and a council that reports to the management board (Figure 4.1). Formalized management, controls and governance are in place. The sustainability working group meets on a monthly basis. It consists of the sustainability coordinators of the different departments and business units: NS Stations, Operations, Commerce and Development, HR, communications and stakeholder management (including brand), procurement, finance and risk, as well as the sustainability team with its different functions. These coordinators each know their department or business unit best, so working with them helps to assess how sustainability can best be embedded in that part of the business.

The relevant departments to engage will differ over time and for each company. In other companies, R&D, product development & innovation, strategy, internal logistics, operations and QHSE (quality, health, safety and environment) might be the most relevant departments to engage.

The Council meets on a quarterly basis. Its consistence changes over time, in sync with the organization of the company. In 2019, it consisted of the directors of business units and staff departments. Within the board of the directors, the CEO is formally responsible for sustainability but the Director of Commerce and Development chairs the Council. The Council provides advice and direction for strategy development and decision-making by the management board.

In addition to the formal structures, there are also many informal meetings and activities to increase the support of sustainability with employees.

Employees are actively encouraged to share their sustainability-related suggestions via regular processes. Further details on generating support are
shared in Chapter 5.

FIGURE 4.1 **NS organizational structure with an overlay of the sustainability matrix structure**

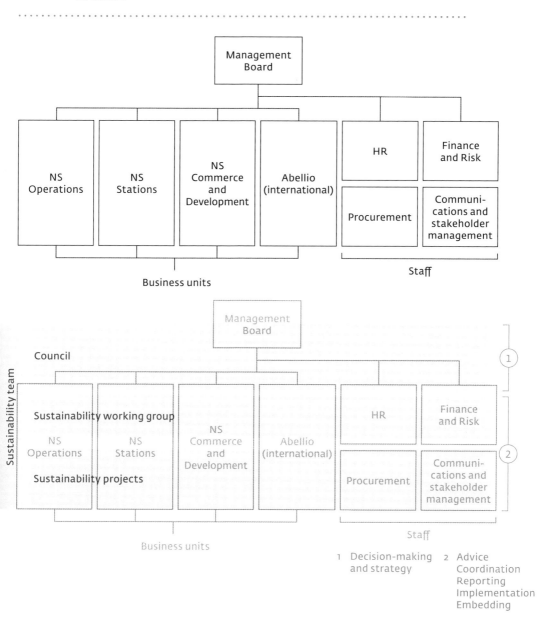

The sustainability department at NS

The first temporary NS sustainability staff department consists of three people, including the sustainability manager. In the past years, this team has focused on:

■ Strategy and embedment in the organization, including governance and reporting
■ Support for business units and staff departments with, for example, knowledge and training
■ Stimulating process on sustainability topics by, for example, sharing knowledge and coordination
■ Development of sustainable innovations with third parties such as suppliers and ProRail
■ Internal and external communications and dialogues, including those with stakeholders.

The department worked across all 7 Roles, which are highlighted in this book. The roles have been translated into three jobs:

■ *Business consultant*: specifies and translates sustainability to the various functions in the primary, supporting and management processes of the organization. Integration takes place based on the structure and management of the organization (strategy, structure, systems) and in part based on the insights and craftsmanship of the employees. They are coached to make tangible how they can contribute to the sustainability goals from their own expertise and role. The business consultant acts mostly as a Mentor, Coordinator and Monitor.
■ *Innovation program manager*: supports the commercial and communications teams, among others, with research and innovations through pilots aimed at creating value from sustainability. The innovation program manager acts as the Innovator, the Coordinator and the Initiator.
■ *Director of sustainability*: sparks the organization to further embed sustainability in the organization. Pro-actively signals external, long-term sustainability developments that could be relevant for the corporate strategy. Connects these developments to the internal organization from a multidisciplinary and holistic view and translates them to opportunities and risks. The director of sustainability acts as the Networker, the Strategist, the Stimulator/Connector and the Initiator.

Currently, the department is organized around the changing needs of the organization, that is, more specific expertise and temporary program management on the strategic themes of climate-neutrality and circular economy. Since the more generic activities of the business consultant and innovation program manager are embedded, these roles are largely replaced by the new expert roles. In this way, the number of staff is still limited to three.

The budget holder decides

The sustainability department's budget is limited. It is usually spent on co-financing of projects, research, communications and training.

This limited budget was an important strategic decision intended to speed up the integration in the business. The starting point is to first find a business owner and split costs to a maximum of 50% financed by the sustainability department to ensure ownership is left with the existing organization. The expectation is that this works better than a set-up with a large sustainability budget and team initiating projects outside of the existing organization, which eventually, would have to be transferred back into the organization.

This decision also has negative consequences as, in a large organization, a limited budget can undermine the credibility or standing within the organization. It also takes time to ensure budget is allocated by other departments. And it is more challenging to direct and influence the course of action if it is not your own budget or team.

Regarding the budget, the same question always comes up: how much should we invest in sustainability? That can be a tough question when the payback period for regular investments is three to five years. In the Dutch context, the environmental law was on our side, requiring companies to implement energy saving measures with a payback period of less than five years. Some companies even stretch the payback period for sustainability investment to ten years or longer. But even then, it is a challenge to allocate resources for investments in sustainability.

Embedding sustainability in the entire (global) organization

When sustainability objectives can be achieved through a limited number of projects, then usually only a limited number of the employees are involved as well. Further integration can be achieved by embedding sustainability into different support systems such as procurement, client services or HR; for example, by including sustainability criteria in the terms and conditions for procurement, behavioral codes, and templates for investment proposals and appraisals. While doing so — translating the sustainability framework to business — this might be more complicated for multinationals located in many different countries and regions because of local legislation or circumstances. Another challenge to a global Coordinator role is that, if different sustainability teams work all over the company, it can be hard to coordinate all initiatives. Much more focus on the "informal" roles, such as Stimulator & Connector or Mentor roles, is then needed to deal with this complexity and eventually embed it in formal processes.

"As a global sustainability manager, I see that our countries perform on different maturity levels of sustainability. Some are still focusing on volunteering, while others are integrating it in the business. However, in every country the sustainability manager recognizes the 7 Roles and finds them very helpful in professionalizing the job of a sustainability manager. The Mentor role is particularly crucial to empowering both the country's sustainability managers and the other employees to reach our sustainability goals. But also, the role as a Stimulator & Connector helps in activating others to integrate sustainability objectives into their jobs. I organized an internal international sustainability meeting that was kicked off by our CEO, a great intervention in my role of Stimulator. But eventually every role is necessary to move the organization to the next level of mature sustainability. The ultimate goal of Randstad is to touch the work lives of 500 million people worldwide, by 2030. I'm confident that the roles will help me and the local sustainability managers to guide Randstad towards this goal!"

MARLOU LEENDERS, GLOBAL SUSTAINABILITY MANAGER RANDSTAD NV

Even at NS, with its focus on the Netherlands, but with operations in Germany and UK, the international complexity holds. The conditions, type and scope of these concessions are different so that the impact and ability to make a change is also different. To give an example, in some concessions, the trains are owned by another party, so that it is more complicated to make energy-saving adjustments. Other ways and means need to be found to reach the set goals.

4.3 The learning Coordinator & Initiator

Search for effective interventions

At NS, we have included sustainability in an optional e-learning module which is offered to all new train and service staff. But if there is little time or willingness to use it, the effect is limited. The same holds for the template for investment proposals that includes a section on sustainability. It was hardly used. On the contrary, many managers were willing to deliver the sustainability data on a quarterly and yearly basis, when asked for, on the same timeline and through the same processes as the financial metrics.

It shows that the ultimate effect of the Coordinator role is very much dependent on finding effective interventions.

Apart from this, as a CSO you have to deal with the pace of change of your organization. This might be slower than the pace of change that you would like, or need, to obtain the sustainability goals. If such is the case, the following interventions might help you to achieve acceleration:

- Expand the Initiating role by carrying out projects or starting activities yourself (as discussed in paragraph 4.1 of this chapter)
- Position the sustainability department at a place in the organization where you can exert the most influence
- Set up a good information system to proactively put sustainability on the decision-making tables
- Deploy professionals with the skills required for acceleration.

The two latter interventions are explained below.

Inside information

Many organizations choose to manage sustainability from a strategic (holding) position in the organization. At NS, the organization of sustainability was not structured as a staff department at the holding company, but as a matrix. The sustainability department was functionally managed by the board member who is responsible for sustainability on the board but hierarchically posted in the largest business unit, under the finance director. As a result, I have received a great deal of information that made faster embedding possible. To give you an example, if the organization started investing in workplaces or trains earlier than anticipated, sustainability specifications could still be included upfront. In addition, in the business unit itself you are closer to the operations — where sustainability is put into action — and you can more easily start conversations about sustainability during management meetings. When I was temporarily unable to participate in the management team of finance, I immediately noticed an information backlog, which meant that I missed the introduction of a new strategy planning process. Good inside information can also be organized informally by making agreements with colleagues to keep you informed or by networking at meetings yourself. In this way you can ensure that sustainability is included in business activities on time.

Professionalization

The development of certain competencies in the team or the addition of professionals with certain competencies can also lead to an acceleration. I have used this opportunity too little. When setting up the sustainability organization, I mainly focused on relevant job areas and business units. I have not consciously been involved with the roles and competencies of employees in the matrix organization and the department. We started with the employees who were already active in this area. No job profiles have been created either. In addition, no uniform agreements have been made with the direct managers of employees in the matrix organization regarding assessment, personal development and training. Not only does this give the sustainability organization a less professional image, but opportunities for personal development can also be missed. The consequences of this in terms of effectiveness are difficult to indicate, but it is certainly worthwhile putting together or developing the most optimal, diverse team in terms of drivers, know-how, competencies and roles.

4.4 The successful Coordinator & Initiator

The best practices of a successful Coordinator show that this role is very much linked to the Monitor role. Instruments like Life Cycle Analysis (LCA) and maturity assessment provide guidance on how to organize and define sustainability in your organization. The following practices describe how the Coordinator role can effectively make use of sustainability information. The working of different measuring instruments such as LCA, (external) uses and collection of sustainability information are further explained in Chapter 8.

Focus and organize sustainability in accordance with the largest impacts
Michael Kobori is former VP Sustainability at Levi Strauss & Co. He developed and led the company's sustainability strategy which included integrating sustainability into all global functions and regional businesses. He started this role in 2001 as a Director Global Code of Conduct for the Chief Supply Chain Officer. In that role, he developed and implemented the company's vendor code of conduct at over 500 supplier locations globally. In the first years, corporate sustainability at Levi's was a "one person department", with focus on labor standards and first-tier suppliers. Since then, the scope of responsibilities and resources has evolved as corporate sustainability has evolved. After a few years the environment, health, and safety department was added and both social and environmental aspects of sustainability were addressed.

Michael:

"The process of transformation of the scope of corporate sustainability was accelerated by the outcome of our environmental product life cycle analysis (E-PLCA). It turned out that the largest impact of our product was not in the first-tier suppliers, but in the raw materials — growing cotton — and consumer use."

Accordingly, the organization of sustainability evolved. In 2019, Michael held the Chair of the company's sustainability board, which includes business leaders from all key functions. He led a global team of twenty-seven sustainability professionals with budget of $5.1 million to manage all value chain labor, environmental, health and safety standards and programs. He reported to the Executive Vice-President and Chief Product and Supply Chain Officer.

Use self-assessment to determine your next step

Maturity models can help determine your next step. They show how far sustainability is embedded and which subsequent steps must be taken. NS self-assessment determines how far it has progressed, based on the activities that have been undertaken. This is an average for the entire company. It is possible that different parts of the company are at a different maturity level. It is interesting to show this as well: this way you can achieve acceleration with the "laggards". In Figure 4.2, you see a maturity model inspired by the Gearing Up Framework of Avastone Consulting (introduced in Chapter 3). It shows the maturity of CSR in the organization in five steps in a more detailed manner than the three steps used in the beginning of this chapter to explain the organization of sustainability. Each of the five steps has its own underlying activities. The first step is compliance with laws and regulations, the last step realizes system changes to eliminate "unsustainability". NS is, on average, between steps 3 and 4. There are activities, among other things, in energy saving and reputation improvement, and a number of suppliers are involved in "greening" the customer's journey. In Figure 4.2, the next steps to achieving further maturity are shown, including further embedding in communication with customers and employees and further development — alone or with partners — of commercial propositions for the consumer market. Italic represents where the expectations are good or where steps have already been taken, such as integrating CSR into the procurement processes and the integrating of social impact in investment decision-making so that decision-making is not only based on financial values, but also on social and ecological values.

There are several maturity models with varying degrees of depth such as the model from the book *Managing the Transition to a Sustainable Enterprise*.[9] This book contains a short questionnaire, on the basis of which you can assess the maturity phase of your organization. A great way to get a more objective determination of your maturity level is to have questionnaires filled in by different people or departments.

Introducing carbon fees to accelerate business ownership

When it comes to sustainability at Microsoft, the partner for business is the Chief Environmental Strategist (CES), comparable with a Chief Sustainability Officer at other companies. The CES is coordinating all initiatives on a corporate level, challenges the business managers with ambitious goals and

FIGURE 4.2 **Maturity Model** (inspired by the Gearing Up Framework of Avastone Consulting)

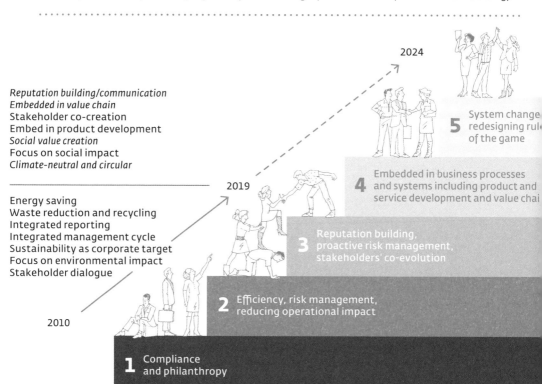

Reputation building/communication
Embedded in value chain
Stakeholder co-creation
Embed in product development
Social value creation
Focus on social impact
Climate-neutral and circular

5 System change redesigning rule of the game

2019

4 Embedded in business processes and systems including product and service development and value chai

Energy saving
Waste reduction and recycling
Integrated reporting
Integrated management cycle
Sustainability as corporate target
Focus on environmental impact
Stakeholder dialogue

3 Reputation building, proactive risk management, stakeholders' co-evolution

2 Efficiency, risk management, reducing operational impact

2010

1 Compliance and philanthropy

2024

monitors the progress that has been made by the business. Business directors are responsible for developing and implementing strategies to obtain the goals. In this way, sustainability is embedded in the core activities of all of Microsoft's business groups. A very effective instrument to accelerate business ownership is the internal carbon fee because — if the fee is high enough — it holds business divisions financially responsible for reducing their carbon emissions. The CES is responsible for the execution of the internal carbon fee. This fee — established by Microsoft in 2012 — is handed down to all of its business groups. It is based on all carbon emissions from energy consumption, including travel.

Renewable energy — wind for the trains — Coordinator & Initiator role

When establishing goals, NS usually adheres to the golden rule: "underpromise and overdeliver". Yet, regarding the goals to use renewable energy for all trains, we deviated from this credo. By establishing a very ambitious goal we wanted to show that we are very serious in our ambition and initiate movement in the market, even if we did not know up front whether we could achieve this goal.

Real change is hardly ever delivered by yourself, so sometimes it is necessary to set goals that you know you cannot reach alone. That is the way to set others in motion. This challenging way of working also fits well with the Stimulator & Connector role of the sustainability manager, which is covered in Chapter 5.

The goal was not only ambitious in terms of timelines and volume — the production of renewable energy at that time was only 4% of national energy production, and the trains use more than 1% — but also in principles. The sustainability principles (as shown in Table 4.1) were translated to the following requirements:

- Renewable energy had to be generated in new renewable power generation plants, as NS did not want to take up existing renewable energy capacity
- This renewable energy had to be traceable to specific power generation plants, from which the electricity for the trains would be supplied
- These new power plants had to be connected to the grid from which the trains derive their power. They would supply the same amount of renewable energy to this grid as would be used by the trains over a year's period. Of this volume, a substantial part had to be generated in the Netherlands. Later this was specified as 50% of the volume.

Aligning decision-making processes
In Europe, tender processes for public sectors are subject to regulations creating level playing fields for market parties. Due to these regulations, in requesting market parties to come up with offers, you have to deal with specific terms, timing and transparent decision-making procedures. Aligning those terms with internal decision-making processes and that of other railway companies participating in the project, requires an extremely precise organization of terms of references of the different actors. Thinking ahead about the request for proposals, the terms of the partnership and also the implementation of this in practice was essential in order to get upfront commitment from the decision-making actors involved. Many documents were drafted beforehand to avoid surprises in the realization phase of the project. Board commitment and support were created in the Strategic role by a strong business case and clear climate-neutral strategy. Subsequently, in the Coordinator role, to bring it further to implementation, a project organization was set up with different scopes, know-how and terms of reference:

- Core team
- Project group (including core team, relevant business owners and staff) and board
- Stakeholder management and communications team
- Steering committee (also representing the other railway companies)
- External advisory experts

This might seem very complex but, for NS, it turned out to be working well in practice and a key success factor, since it captured both the expertise to trigger innovative offers and movement in the market, and enough internal leverage to finally get the desired approvals.

Tips for Coordinators & Initiators

- Ensure that what the organization needs to achieve is crystal clear.
- Find an owner for each topic and objective, so it is clear who is responsible and for what.
- Translate the objectives towards the entire organization, so everyone can contribute through concrete action and innovation. Do not just set objectives for the largest polluters.
- Change an "underpromise and overdeliver culture" into a "smart risk-taking culture" when it comes to sustainability.
- Make use of existing methods for strategic planning and implementation. Based on those methods, determine what you will organize centrally and what you will leave to other departments.
- If you want to achieve results or showcase innovations fast(er), consider carrying out a few sustainability projects yourself as the sustainability manager/ team, as long as you keep involving the existing organization.
- Force the existing organization to actively engage by funding a maximum of 50% from the sustainability budget.
- If you cannot find a business owner within three years for a project that you initiated, you should stop the project.
- Be aware that a company is always in the process of changing. This can pose opportunities and risks.
- Be alert to changes in strategy, structure systems and, where necessary, adjust the sustainability organization to ensure effective integration.
- Use patience and intuition to determine when to go with the flow and when not.
- Adjust the structure and the position of the sustainability team as needed to further make your company more sustainable.
- Understand how your company works and whom or what you need to get things done.
- For multinationals consider local conditions.
- Establish a good flow of information, both formally and informally.
- Do not just involve those people willing to contribute, but also the people you really need; for example, those with the relevant knowledge and competencies.
- Professionalize the sustainability organization with job profiles, competencies, and agreements for appraisal and development meetings.
- Use a maturity model to assess the progress you have made and where you would like to take your organization.
- Trigger business ownership with effective instruments that holds them directly responsible for their impact, such as the introduction of an internal carbon fee.

Based on his experiences, Michaels Kobori's advice to other CSOs is to:

- Do your homework: do an environmental life cycle analysis and understand where your impacts are; do a materiality assessment to find your most relevant material issues (as described in the Monitor and Networker role)
- Understand the language of finance since this is the most important department if you want to achieve results
- Be the three P's that Bob Langert (former VP Sustainability of McDonalds) mentions in his book *The Battle to Do Good*: Patience, Passion, Perseverance, and then add the C of Charm. In the Coordinator role, a CSO should be a catalyst!

The Stimulator & Connector

"A leader is best
When people barely know he exists,
When his work is done, his aim fulfilled,
They will say, 'We did this ourselves'."

LAO TZU, CHINESE PHILOSOPHER AND AUTHOR OF THE TAO TE CHING

The sustainability or CSR professional is an ambassador for the field of sustainability. His or her personal ideals and ways of working are based on sustainability principles. In that way (s)he motivates, stimulates, inspires and activates others to integrate sustainability objectives into their roles. The CSR, sustainability manager or CSO builds bridges between the outside and the inside. (S)he connects things in ways to speed up more sustainable business practices and usually achieves this without formal authority, so (s)he has to generate support for change towards a more sustainable organization in different ways.

"People aspire to have a meaningful
role, contributing to a higher purpose.
Supporting them in discovering how they

can link their aspirations to the company goals is key. As a company, building upon the expertise and passion of a person unleashes creativity and leads to innovation. It engages and drives people in a way you cannot formally organize."

GEANNE VAN ARKEL (HEAD OF SUSTAINABLE DEVELOPMENT FOR DESIGNER AND MAKER OF MODULAR FLOORING, INTERFACE IN EUROPE)

Generating support is crucial for the CSO or CSR manager's success. Sustainable business is all about changing people and their behavior. One of the key questions raised by sustainability managers is: how do I create support for sustainability with employees and the board? This is a double-edged challenge, as to generate support from employees and senior management, commitment is crucial. This chapter addresses this question through tips and insights.

5.1 Why does sustainability need support?

If there is insufficient support and the responsibility and initiative are left with a very limited number of people, then there is a risk of the sustainability strategy evaporating with just a few personnel changes. The more employees feel engaged, the better sustainability will be embedded and the higher the profile of sustainability will be. In that case, sustainability does not just depend on the sustainability team and a handful of engaged employees.

How do you generate support and how do you ensure a successful implementation of the sustainability strategy? According to Professor André Nijhof of Nyenrode Business University, research shows that 40% depends on structural elements like reporting, checklists, e-learnings tool, codes of conduct and audits. That leaves 60% dependent on the organizational culture, the mindset and behavior of the employees.

The Stimulator & Connector role of the CSR manager focuses on these non-structural elements, like the culture and the behavior of people within the organization. One of the key challenges in this role is to create an undercurrent of new ideas within your organization and stimulate employees to implement these ideas themselves. For successful integration of sustainability, you need initiatives and enthusiasm from employees. Implementation of the strategy depends on their sustainable behavior at the operational level and ideas on how the company can become more sustainable. This undercurrent of new ideas and sustainable behavior does not happen spontaneously.

According to Diane Holdorf:

"The key to success for a CSO is leading through influence — being business savvy."

As CSO of Kellogg Company, she spent most of her time in the Stimulator & Connector role, which she would rather call an integrator and capacity builder role: understanding the business objective, building trust and support — which can sometimes be lost when teams change — creating crucial (supply chain) and cross-functional connections to embed sustainability into operations and (marketing) strategies.

The Stimulator role differs from the Coordinator role (Chapter 4) in focus and type of activities. In the Coordinator role, the sustainability manager is primarily focused on the structural aspects of integration. These structural interventions are often initiated by or with senior management and reach the employees in a top-down fashion. The Stimulator role focuses on the cultural aspects, generating support without formal instruments and promoting sustainability in every department. An important tool for creating this undercurrent is (embedding) a clear corporate purpose, defined by answering Simon Sinek's question: "Why do we do what we do?," as discussed in Chapter 3 on the Strategic role.

Both roles are needed, complimentary and reinforcing. A successful implementation of sustainability requires a fine balance between these roles: balancing structure, culture and behavior. Because of their reinforcing nature to generate support, both roles are often considered as one role.

The next conditions (both structural and cultural elements), help to create the optimal conditions to be effective in the Stimulator role:
- Senior management support of sustainable business. So, generating (or maintaining) support from senior management requires real attention from the CSR manager. The underlying intentions or why (purpose) of senior management needs to be clear, promoted and embedded in every department, so employees can feel connected to what senior management stands for.
- A vision in which the why — or the need — for sustainability is established. Translated to a strategic framework or principles, it then becomes clear what sustainability means for the company and how it can be achieved.
- Key external and internal stakeholders have been engaged in the creation of and/or decision-making on the vision and strategy to build a supportive coalition.

- Sustainability is organized in such a way that it triggers initiatives from within the existing organization and leaves the responsibility for implementation there as well. Sustainability is embedded in select organizational systems and processes, such as the strategic planning cycle, templates for investment proposals, job description, code of conduct, etc. The 40% of the structural elements need to be in order quite visibly, ensuring sustainability is constantly top of mind throughout the organization.
- The CSR or sustainability manager acts in an open, social and communicative manner, which facilitates the organization and creates goodwill. (S)he provides others with the opportunity to contribute and offer suggestions.
- The CSR or sustainability manager makes drivers or intentions behind employee behaviors visible; for example, by initiating open conversations with them. (S)he connects them to the underlying intentions (purpose of the company) of the sustainability strategy.
- The CSR or sustainability manager creates a sustainable "winning team" undercurrent in the organization by, for example:
  - Providing a stage to colleagues who have achieved results. This way people internalize the story, they become proud and also inspire others.
  - Or, bringing an external point of view into the organization (through a peer or an important stakeholder) to support a key argument or to inspire from another perspective, such as bringing in another CEO to share an inspiring sustainability story.

But support is not all you need. Once employees know and understand what sustainability means for the company, it also needs to become clear what they can do themselves within the scope of their own roles: and they need to be able to do so. Translating sustainability to specific functions in the

TABLE 5.1 **Reinforcing roles (in practice often combined) to generate support and action**

Roles	Description of the role
Coordinator and Initiator Support and catalyze implementation	Support people in other departments in the organization to implement the sustainability strategy **using the governance/organizational structure**. You work with many others to create an (integrated) *plan, to embed* it into the organization and to set things in motion. Initially it might include starting up iconic projects yourself.
Stimulator and Connector Challenge **to inspire** and connect	Act as a sustainability ambassador, inspiring (outside-in) and activating others to integrate sustainability goals into tasks, usually **without formal influence**. This is all about *generating support* within the organization.
Mentor Empower others for success	**On an individual functional level**: advise, inform and train colleagues, to enable them to achieve the sustainability goals. This is all about *translating sustainability to the daily reality of the workplace* of each team.

organization is covered in the Mentor role in Chapter 6. Table 5.1 — a cut out of the 7 Roles model — lists the descriptions of the three reinforcing roles.

Communicate, communicate, communicate

To generate support among employees, it is clear that you can never "over-communicate" on sustainability. When it comes to effective communication, the tone at the top, credibility, relevance, and repetition are all important. The following tips can be helpful to boost the impact of your sustainability communications.

TONE AT THE TOP

- Enable senior leadership to frequently and actively speak on the importance of sustainability inside and outside the organization. Organize communications materials, briefing documents and stages for such talks.

CREDIBILITY

- Always communicate intentions and drivers, not just results. Employees feel a stronger connection to the "why" of the company or the strategy, rather than the results and how they were achieved.
- Be consistent in your sustainability messaging as an organization. You undermine your own credibility if you are saying one thing, but doing the other. For example, in the past, NS talked about considering waste as a valuable resource, but this was before separate trash cans were available at all train stations.
- All sustainability measures also need to be visibly implemented at the board level, to make the tone at the top credible. They need to lead by example, such as working with fewer or no printers and separating their trash.

RELEVANCE

- Communicating is hard work. It is essential to prepare well for each communications opportunity, whether it is a one-on-one meeting or a presentation to a room filled with three hundred people. Decide up front what you want to achieve, what your key message will be and how you work towards it; always keep in mind what you want the audience to do afterwards. An easy pitfall is to try to include too much in your story. Usually it works better to focus on a key message, supported by relevant examples.
- Choose carefully the projects you want to communicate: they will not all be equally relevant. Projects are more relevant when they are appealing, impactful, democratically decided and supported by management.
- Next to hard work, self-reflection and humor are a must.

REPETITION

- In sustainability communications, repetition is key. Even though there are people who say they are fully aware, the majority will keep asking why we do not share the positive sustainable news more often. To structurally repeat key messages, make use of internal communications channels like the intranet and reserve space for sustainability news on these platforms. Within the building, think of communicating in places that employees pass frequently during the day, such as stickers near light switches, signs in the elevators and updates near the coffee stations. Alternately, use external channels that are frequently visited by your colleagues like, LinkedIn.

- Repeatedly use the same concise model or visual. This way you can indicate where something fits in at a higher level and yet make it more concrete and easier to understand. The temple model is frequently used for this, with the vision as the roof of the temple, supported by different pillars of the strategy and a foundation of sustainability principles. The strategic cube (Figure 3.6) is another example of a strong visual that is used to tell a story.

- For many people, the terms "sustainability" and "CSR" are meaningless. Carefully consider the most relevant terms to use and spend time clarifying what you mean.

The internal sustainability network

Chapter 2 highlighted how to increase internal support through the engagement of external stakeholders. But you also need internal support from people at key positions in the organization. These people can offer informal support when things do not progress through the formal channels and can also be key sparring partners to help define how to continue and progress.

As mentioned in Chapter 4, an effective internal network can provide valuable information to you in your Coordinator role: information to which you may not always have access through the formal channels. For generating support, access to information is crucial. In large organizations — where you cannot possibly be aware of everything — your internal network can share information in an informal way on new opportunities to integrate sustainability. This can be the start of procurement or developing corporate brand processes as well as lower-impact but highly visible processes, such as introducing sustainable catering at venues for events.

The internal support network — especially in other business units in different regions or countries — provide extra sets of eyes and ears, making them crucial in driving sustainable change. They can give you feedback and information about what is really going on. And while they are intrinsically motivated, they usually also become the first sustainability working group or steering committee. This is a way to formalize their sustainability role.

Sustainable behavior

Even when everyone understands the "why" and the "what" and says they will act more sustainably, it does not mean that people will actually do so. Behavioral science provides useful insights to understand more about human behavior. An important insight is that most of our behavior (approximately 90%) is determined unconsciously, as if on autopilot. Only a small portion of our behavior is consciously determined by us. And that is okay, as the people functioning best are those able to automate much of their behavior. To survive, people need to delegate much to the unconscious. So, when trying to change behaviors, it is important to know which are the drivers underneath the unconscious behaviors.

Drivers which kept us alive millions of years ago still exist, more or less. In essence, we are all social creatures, going for short-term gains. Maintaining a positive self-image is another important driver. It explains some of the unexpected and sometimes emotional responses to the topic of sustainability. The normative charge of the term sustainability can have an unintended effect on the other's positive self-image. If you do not act sustainably, you are not doing the right thing (and I am doing just that). It is important to take that into consideration when communicating about sustainability. You need to communicate in a way without an implied value judgment. Especially people with a strong intrinsic motivation can come across as highly normative, risking a reduction — rather than an increase — in support for sustainability.

In addition to a positive self-image, other factors that influence behavior change are, competition, direct feedback, ease and habits. Unilever captures this nicely in its model, the five levers for change:
- Make it understood (awareness and acceptance)
- Make it easy (convenience and confidence)
- Make it desirable (self and society)
- Make it rewarding (proof and payoff)
- Make it a habit (reinforcing and reminding).

The lever, "make it desirable", is particularly directed at the positive self-image. Unilever's model has been designed to change consumer behavior, but it also applies to creating sustainable behavior in companies. Consider using these levers in your activities and communications.

Corporate values

It is a challenge to really understand a company and its dynamics. What are the basic elements of our company's culture? What are the values of our company? Is there only one set of values, or does everyone have their own version of a company's values? Can a company's values be used to embed sustainable behavior? The answer to these questions depends very much on the type of company and the way you use the dynamics of the company to embed sustainability. Values can be a strong compass towards a sustainable business strategy, especially when they originate from their founders and are embedded in the mission or purpose, as can be seen with companies such as Interface and Tommy Hilfiger. However, other symbolic forms and activities accumulated over time shape an organization's unique identity and character. Often a company cherishes its own myths, rituals and even humor. Involving so-called company heroes to generate support for sustainability plans can be very effective.

Again, it is the job of the sustainability manager to really understand the dynamics of his or her company: to do so takes time, knowledge and different perspectives. In their book, Reframing Organizations, organizational behavior experts Lee G. Bolman and Terrence E. Deal, offer four "frames" through which one can analyze organizations, procedures and dynamics at work. Over the years, many books on the subject have been published; however, to come up with a plan, you have to understand your company from practice - being on the work floor asking questions and really listening. Or as John le Carré says:

"A desk is a dangerous place from which to view the world."

5.2 Generating support in practice

Asking many of questions and really listening to the answers helps to generate support. There are many reasons why employees do or do not want to behave more sustainably. One reason is not better than the other. By asking questions, you uncover what is really on people's minds and what drives them. That understanding will help to find a trigger to support them to get started. This could be related to their profession, to doing things together with others, or to create that better world. Sometimes the willingness might be there, but there are practical obstacles that get in the way, such as limited time or capacity. If you discover the obstacles and help to overcome them — for example, by temporarily taking on a task or educating colleagues — then you can create the support needed for sustainable change. With others, it might be a lack of inspiration, which can be overcome by showing the approach of other companies or organizing more sustainable business practices. In sum, there are different ways to increase acceptance of behavior change. As the sustainability manager, you have to be quite flexible to be an effective Stimulator & Connector.

Estimating what the other needs is usually quite an intuitive process. Be careful not to want to go too fast, but to really listen to others and to explore what they or the situation really require. Your own personal drive and sense of urgency can get in the way. If you go too fast, others might not be willing, or able, to follow and could disconnect. Such a questioning conversation is very valuable when it comes to generating support from key people in the organization, such as senior management and middle management. It enables you to tailor your approach and to do what is needed to engage them.

Obviously, you cannot have such a personal conversation with each and every person in the organization, especially in a large company with thousands of employees. Yet you can translate this approach into a more general principle to adhere to: always strive to really understand your target group. Learn to speak their language, understand their arguments and connect with their needs and desires. A competitive analysis will likely resonate with the sales department, while pride and employee engagement will speak to the HR department. Finding the right "hook" with each target group requires the CSR manager to understand and be sensitive to the language and culture of the different functions and teams in the organization.

"The best tip I have for (beginning) CSOs — and probably all other professionals — is that it is important to be 'light', be optimistic, always find or celebrate a win. People like spending time with positive people. If people like interacting with you, there is a greater chance that people will actually do what you ask. So, my most effective intervention is to use my charm, every day!"

MICHAEL KOBORI (FORMER VP SUSTAINABILITY AT LEVI STRAUSS & CO.)

What's in it for them?

To understand what sustainability meant to my colleagues in the NS Operations business unit, I organized a Sustainability Tour. Together with a few colleagues, armed with a rolling case filled with information materials, a sustainability quiz and an inspiring video, I went on tour to talk to people at many railway stations and offices. A key conclusion was that sustainability fits well with the craftsmanship of many of my (former) colleagues. Also, it is important to offer a very concrete call to action, like energy-efficient driving (eco-driving) for the train drivers. Thanks to the tour, we collected many ideas for improvement, which showed deep engagement. Most of these ideas were picked up by employees themselves, such as more energy-efficient machines in canteens or reducing the waste caused by the use of paper and paper cups. Finally, it became very clear that everyone has personal norms. What is very natural for one person, like turning the lights off when you leave the office, may require a behavioral change for another.

Establishing and maintaining internal support is key to the role of the Stimulator & Connector. You can do this by taking stock through your network of whether there are people or groups already working on sustainable change. Peer communications is really effective, so on each floor you can have volunteers to support colleagues with tips for campaigns like making your workplace more sustainable. These volunteers are all intrinsically motivated and eager to contribute. In addition, at NS, a group of young professionals — calling themselves "coffee guerillas" — successfully introduced reusable coffee cups in offices.

Via internal communications, people can be encouraged to submit sustainable ideas. To maintain internal support, consider up front how you can act on these ideas. Otherwise, such a call to action could lose credibility and even lead to disappointments. What worked well at NS is to align this process with existing idea management systems and competitions in the organization.

Most people in the internal sustainability network at NS are solid opinion leaders, who really believe in the need for more sustainable business practices and who can therefore uphold their conviction in all circumstances. In change theory, these people are sometimes referred to as the strategic coalition. Their engagement is fueled by publicly sharing their achievements (big and small) during informal events. From the start in my sustainability role at NS, I have been fortunate in being able to count on a number of reliable and active internal supporters. To this date, they continue to support the sustainability activities, both formally and informally.

Just do it

Of course, there are other ways to steer employees towards desired behavior in organizations. You can also just do it or try something out; for example, the waste management process at the NS offices. Previously, there were trash cans next to all desks, but these were removed to encourage people to separate their waste. At central locations throughout the offices, waste separation stations were placed. The situation was changed overnight, outside of office hours, and no real effort was made to communicate this change up front. After two, three weeks, the new situation and the changed behavior was well established, simply because there were no other options available.

Another example of "just do it" was the introduction of reusable water bottles in the office of Google in order to reduce the use of plastic bottles. The side effect of this introduction however, was that workers were drinking less water than before, which is not healthy. So, the sustainability department had to come up with a different solution that met both goals: reducing negative environmental impact and a healthy worker. The solution was the introduction of the refilled reusable bottles, which made it easier and the water drinking levels went back to normal.

5.3 The learning Stimulator & Connector

Management engagement

The structural elements addressed in the Coordinator role can be a first step in awareness and broadening knowledge with management. At least it ensures that sustainability is discussed. Inclusion of sustainability in the so-called target letters of higher management, sustainability KPIs in scorecards or in the procurement processes, are examples that often start discussions. Therefore, an important learning moment is that structural elements can open the door a little, but actual support is only created if you can really make the other person enthusiastic.

For this you have to be aware of underlying motives, appeal to craftsmanship, make impact visible and/or show appealing examples of innovations. Nevertheless, it is always a challenge to maintain support and attention for long-term sustainable goals, because the daily activities already require more attention, especially with middle management.

This challenge also became clear when I was CSO at NS. Once every two years, employee engagement in sustainability was measured, following the regular employee engagement survey. The repetitive conclusions of the measurements were:
- Much still needs to be explained about sustainable business practices at NS
- Communication contributes to knowledge and attitude but not to a change in behavior.

What was striking in the research is that managers did not show the pioneering role that was expected of them. In fact, they scored lower than other employees. The explanation could be that the daily attention of the manager goes to operational implementation and, as long as there is a need for improvement in this area, there is little appetite for doing things in a more sustainable way. Despite this explanation, the outcome led me to instruct a number of young professionals to investigate further. According to them, the main cause of the low score of managers was the unclear internal positioning of sustainability at NS, such as the different ways in which sustainability was included in business plans, assessment forms, job profiles and investment decisions. In short, it was mainly caused by the absence of part of the 40% structural elements.

Often, if things in daily activities are not going well, sustainability becomes an "add-on" instead of another, inspiring way of working. Or to put it more strongly, as long as the other basic activities are not yet in order, sustainability is seen as a luxury. The idea behind this is that sustainability or social responsibility is a kind of luxury that a company can afford in good times but that is quickly scrapped in bad times.

Finding the right mix

An extra difficulty in the Stimulator role is the vulnerability of internal support. As soon as colleagues change jobs or leave the company, their support is gone and you have to start all over again with the new colleague. At NS, for example, at a certain period, many managers changed jobs in a short time. That demanded extra attention from me to ensure internal support, especially with middle management. Again, in such a situation it helps if the structural elements are in order, but it should always be a mix.

According to Brian Janous (General Manager of Energy and Sustainability at Microsoft) the most important tips (for a CSO) to overcome obstacles are:

1   To create executive sponsorship and recognition; it should be in the company or organization's DNA. Key executives sitting together asking themselves the question: "What is it that we want to be?" A CSO need to be "covered" by the board in order to execute. The challenge with sustainability is that there is always a reason not to do it. For Microsoft, sustainability is a value that stands above day-to-day execution and remains the core business priority.

2   To make the CEO accountable; it certainly helps if every business director has to meet its KPIs but, in the end, the CEO is accountable. (S)he should be the one who makes the announcement about new commitments or achievements. For internal focus and engagement, it should be clear that sustainability is part of the president's job. Microsoft's CEO is a great example of this accountability.

3   To look further than one's own company's needs, find new partners and share lessons learned. If we want to accelerate the energy transition, we need to do more than just buy renewable energy. We need to figure out how we can help transform energy markets and decarbonize the grid, meaning that we have to constantly innovate to overcome obstacles. A good example are the new deal structures that are created "to lower risk

and/or lower costs for others to participate in the market, such as the Proxy Revenue Swap or the Volume Firming Agreement (VFA) developed with insurance companies to mitigate weather risks."[10]

4 To use R&D, technology and operations to test new solutions. Microsoft does this with integrated energy-storage batteries in wind turbines, grid-integrated batteries and software, and AI-enabled autonomous grids for utilities serving more renewable loads. More tech companies can/should use their technologies to accelerate transition.

And last but not least, one of the key elements in Brian's success is that he has a solid and appealing story when he explains why renewable energy should be supported:

"Companies have a responsibility and can play a significant role in meeting the needs of society by creating value for customers and stakeholders. Growing the percentage of renewable energy powering operations is a great example of such a value-based perspective. Most corporate procurement of renewables by PPAs (power purchase agreements) deals are good for business as well, a win-win situation."

5.4 The successful Stimulator & Connector

A great example of generating support is "The Fast Forward to 2020" program of Interface –the world's largest designer and maker of carpet tiles. This company offers an advanced training to employees and associates, while a network of sustainability ambassadors helps further development and promotion of "Mission Zero" — Interface's promise to eliminate any negative impact the company may have on the environment by the year 2020 — within the company. This sustainability training program empowers people to use both their expertise and their passion in contributing to the mission of Interface to become a restorative company on three levels:

- Level 1 is an introduction training for new employees understanding what sustainability means for Interface, introducing The Natural Step, Biomimicry and the 7 Fronts. People also share what sustainability means for them, understanding the different aspects.
- Level 2 comprehends a team session on functional level. How can you, as an engineer, marketing team, or operator contribute to the mission of Interface, using your expertise. You ask "the help question", which empowers people in their role.
- When a person is truly motivated (s)he can apply to become a Sustainability Ambassador (Level 3), which is not only a training program with colleagues from different departments, but also includes writing a paper. This paper should be a proposal for a project that contributes to the

Interface mission and should be defended from both a sustainability and economic perspective, so employees learn to "sell" their ideas.

The result is a significant internal involvement among employees at all levels. They are provided with the space to help realize the company's sustainability goals. Through the strategic and inspiring foundation created in the nineties, employees know that they can contribute to a greater purpose which is an important motivation for many current and potential employees. In fact, this program is a combination of the Stimulator and Mentor role. Making sustainability everyone's role resulted in collaboration within the company and throughout the supply chain, creating a stream of innovative products and services and subsequently contributed to a low-carbon circular economy. While celebrating the success of Mission Zero in 2019, the company raised the bar with its mission "Climate Take Back." Interface is working on creating flooring solutions that are climate positive and even have a carbon-negative footprint. The FastForward 2020 program is being adapted to support the regenerative ambition of this 2040 goal, incorporating their lessons learned.[11]

Interface's approach of promoting and embedding a purpose in every department is supported by research done by Professor CB Bhattacharya and published in his book, *Small Actions, Big Difference* (2020)[12]. It suggests that, for creating sustainable success, it is vital to create a sense of "sustainability ownership" with employees and to win over employees' hearts and mind with a shared purpose.

Supportive activities

Support generation can be done in various ways, such as competitions and engaging internal sustainability networks (ambassadors) and volunteers. As mentioned earlier in this chapter, at NS, for example, we introduced green teams of enthusiastic colleagues on each floor level to motivate other colleagues to turn off lights, computers and heat at the end of the working day. To show the effect per floor, a daily detailed report of the energy use of the building was made and a small prize was awarded for the three floors that saved the most energy. The result was unexpected: the energy use of building showed a 15% drop. The extra effect of this competition was that it raised awareness and workers started to ask themselves how sustainability could be integrated into their work.

The informal meetings also helped to generate support, to inspire and challenge employees with ideas and solutions, and to cheer employees who created sustainable successes. The informal meetings would normally be interactive afternoons during working hours, with a varied program where everyone was welcome:

- Inspiring lectures
- Ideas competition
- Network sessions
- Speed dating with board members
- Interactive panel discussion with the public
- Information about the latest sustainable initiatives and results
- Thematic and practice-oriented workshops
- Informational quiz.

With these meetings, my goal was to provide sufficient information and inspiration so that employees could do things differently in their work the next day. I often concluded with the question: what will you do differently tomorrow? After I had organized these meetings a number of times, the organization started to rotate and was taken over by the ambassadors (internal network). The informal meetings also changed forms, such as lunch meetings on sustainability themes.

Social intrapreneurship

A term that you often encounter in the Stimulator & Connector role of CSR managers is "social intrapreneurship". This means that an organization offers space to employees to behave as entrepreneurs in a social way. This can be done in various ways. At NS, we have the so-called "Social Headquarters". This was set up by a group of committed employees who have made agreements with their managers about the required space and time. They come up with projects based on their social involvement and work. An example of this is the donation of public transport rickshaws to people in Bangladesh to build a new life. The rickshaws are financed from the sale of upcycled old train benches or other train materials sold to the public. Social Headquarters is not part of the formal sustainability policy and reporting. As a result, this internal social entrepreneurship is given the space to form and take shape from the bottom up. Another example of social entrepreneurship, are the two days of "RailWish" every year, in which employee volunteers of NS and ProRail put a smile on faces of rail fans by making their "rail wishes" come true. These are wishes of rail fans who can often use a helping hand; for example, a day trip with a conductor, a look at the train driver or a visit to the railway museum. These days were created as part of a management development training. In May 2008, fifteen employees of NS and ProRail organized the "RailWish" days for the first time, in which they mobilized one hundred and fifty volunteers within NS and ProRail to fulfill rail-related wishes. Because of their success, the Initiators decided to turn these "RailWish" days into an annual event and to set up a RailWishDay Foundation.

Foundations

To make a contribution to social projects in a more structured and coordinated way, companies often choose to start a Foundation that supports social projects by donating money or employees' time, or both. This so-called Corporate philanthropy can be important for employee engagement, or recruiting employees that are potentially more socially responsible. Often these Foundations — funded by a small percentage of corporate profits — are run by persons other than the CSO or CSR manager and are subject to a separate governance and social policy.

CSR managers in companies that also have a Corporate Foundation do well to consider the position and orientation of this Corporate Foundation in relation to the activities and goals of the sustainability department. Both focus on the relationship between the organization and (broader) social issues and this might reinforce one another, if goals are aligned. This goes further than stimulating employee engagement, as mentioned before in relation to the socially orientated Foundations. For instance, business-orientated Foundations, using resources for "business-related" projects and activities might motivate the parent company to use its business activities for a social theme. Or system-orientated Foundations might use resources to make a positive change in a system, such as a new, more social working method in a sector, enabling the parent company to be a first mover "system changer".

Renewable energy — wind for the trains — Stimulator & Connector role

My Stimulator & Connector role was very crucial in convincing the internal organization, the external market and stakeholders that we should do things differently when it comes to electricity for the trains. It had never been done before and, especially when we started to do the market research, vested interests found their way to the board, questioning the feasibility of my idea. Electricity is a strategic asset: as a quite substantial part of the budget, it had the attention of both the board and the Supervisory board. Knowing that there would be a great deal of attention at a high level, I used my Network role to attract the support of high-level ambassadors and experts around the most important decision-making actors, using my own professional background and network in the energy markets. Their intervention — asking the "right" questions — and talks with the board and the Supervisory board, helped the idea evolve into a board-approved strategy.
Once the process of purchasing new wind power for the trains had started, I realized that ambitious steps of this kind actually supported my Stimulator role. They have a stimulating and connecting effect on your internal and external stakeholders, and employees discover that this is a project of which they can be proud.

The project shows that sustainability is important in the company and that management is willing to invest in the collective interest, "as shared corporate value". It also feeds those with potential to come up with other sustainable ideas. Those external stakeholders who like to think along with you, see it as an example for themselves or for others and that creates movement. It is therefore of great importance that the appeal of impactful projects is communicated in a clear and effective way, both within the company and externally. Share your dilemmas, share your pride and be open to what is going on. The importance of achieving internal support by involving as many employees as possible is, I believe, overestimated. By that I mean that the impact of realizing relevant projects with a small group of colleagues will naturally inspire other employees. So, focus primarily on those who can and want to make great strides, using your own Initiator and Innovator roles to get appealing projects off the ground.

The impact of appealing projects was also experienced by Janice Lao, Director, Group Corporate Responsibility and Sustainability at the Hongkong and Shanghai Hotels (HSH), which owns and operates the Peninsula Hotels and other luxury real estate around the world, when the Peninsula took shark fin off its menus:

> *"It was amazing — based on very rough estimates from our consultants, around 18,000 hotels around the world followed our lead. Perhaps because of the fact that we are listed in Hong Kong, which is the center of this trade, and we're an iconic brand. I think people were somewhat surprised with the impact we had, as were we."*

Tips for Stimulators & Connectors

- Learn from others how they generate support, learn from their best practices.
- Focus the generation of support on a few key people who want to have and can have real impact. Find and use your "company heroes".
- Consider whose help you need to get something done. This is not confined to managers; people in support roles can have a strong, positive influence.
- If you are just getting started with sustainability as an organization, create a platform to give credits and visibility to those people who achieve sustainable results, based on their intrinsic motivation. This is a great way to start to generate support.
- Be aware that your intrinsic motivation and engagement with sustainability can be a pitfall. If you make it too personal, you may waste much energy and you may try too hard to persuade others.
- A two-minute video of clients talking about how they view sustainability in your company probably has more impact than data and graphs.
- Capture three to five of the most important sustainability facts on the back of your team's business cards, so it is easy to bring them into the conversation.
- You can never over-communicate on sustainability. Take care of the tone at the top, credibility, relevance and repetition.
- Communicate hard, factual and understandable results, preferably verified by a recognized, independent third party.
- Share achievements by colleagues from the entire organization.
- Use humor and search for the "hook" to catch the other's attention. What's in it for them?
- Do not expect miracles from communication. Communication does not automatically lead to behavior change. Engage people, provide insight on their impact and use the five levers of change.
- "Just do it" is a great mantra for some behavioral changes. Simply getting started makes it easier to change and create new habits.
- If you ask for suggestions and ideas from others, make sure you can follow up on them, through existing processes, if possible. This avoids disappointments Create a sense of "sustainability ownership" with employees.
- Be alert to the vulnerability of internal support in a changing organization.
- Use an appealing and relevant project to showcase how important sustainability is to the company.
- Provide space for bottom-up internal social entrepreneurship to flourish.
- Make an effort to really understand your company and its dynamics from different perspectives and to find the right mix of interventions (including structural elements) to build your support for transition.
- If applicable, consider aligning the position and orientation of a Corporate Foundation to sustainability goals.

- Be "light", always find or celebrate a win. If people like interacting with you, there is a greater chance that people will actually do what you ask.
- Dedicate time to your Stimulator & Connector role, but do not let this fully occupy you.

The Mentor

"Tell me and I forget.
Teach me and I remember.
Involve me and I learn."

BENJAMIN FRANKLIN (1706-1790), AMERICAN SCIENTIST AND POLITICIAN

The CSO and sustainability team spend a lot of their time advising, informing and training employees to empower them to reach the sustainability goals that are part of their tasks and role. The CSO or CSR manager becomes a Mentor: gathering information and ensuring that people are informed about and discover the relevance of sustainability to their role and function in the organization.

"As a CSO you have to understand what is truly
motivating and how you can empower
others to lead and be successful. As most
employees are best able to assess how
to integrate sustainability into their
tasks or function, the Mentor role
of the sustainability leader is to
engage others, for example, through
offering support and coaching."

DIANE HOLDORF (FORMER CSO OF KELLOGG COMPANY)

As a Mentor, it is crucial for you to know how to translate sustainability to different functions in the organization and what tools are available to make jobs and tasks more sustainable. You can only support people if

you have some insight into their role and job. You must continuously adjust your "Mentoring style" to different situations and colleagues. Cross-functional experience will help you to make sustainability relevant to people in different functions in your organization.

As Anniek Mauser of Unilever puts it:

> *"You need to know enough about all functions*
> *to be able to make the translation",*

and I think that it is one of the aspects of the job that makes being a CSO so interesting. The difference with the Stimulator role is that the CSO in the Mentor role works on an individual or functional level, whereas the Stimulator role focuses on engaging people on a general organizational level. This chapter about the Mentor role of a CSO covers various ways of introducing sustainability to different departments in the organization. It shows how crucial the Mentoring practices of CSOs are in taking the sustainability maturity of their organizations to the next level.

6.1 Integration of sustainability on a functional level

By analyzing the key business processes and considering which ones will be subject to sustainability-related changes, you can draw up a plan for the further integration of sustainability into the organizational functions. You map those processes in detail and — in close cooperation with relevant managers — consider which will be subject to change. To embed this in the organization, such changes need to be included in handbooks, internal training, appraisal systems, templates, etc. (Figure 6.1).

Through workshops or individual meetings, the CSR manager or team helps an employee to determine how (s)he can contribute in his or her role. This usually generates a long list of potential actions and activities for different functions. These lists of activities provide excellent input for target-setting meetings as part of the appraisal cycle as well as for regular progress updates.

The actual workshop process is just as important as the results of the workshop. Going through such a workshop as a team increases ownership for different results. Workshops also contribute to unconscious drivers of behavior, such as public commitment and peer pressure from colleagues.

In a professional organization, people often understand how to integrate sustainability into their role and some functions develop a different focus

FIGURE 6.1 **Integration of sustainability in organizational processes**

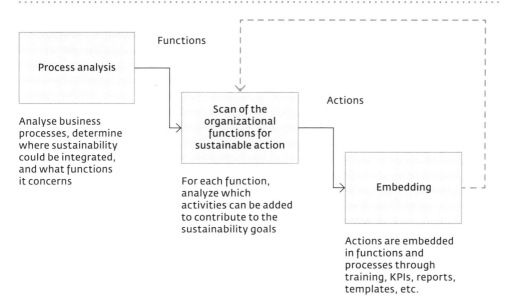

due to the integration of sustainability, which may also require different competencies. For example, procurement professionals will most likely need to rely less on their project management skills, developing much more interpersonal skills to get to joint solutions. The sales professional will be asked to develop some sustainability knowledge, so as to include sustainability aspects of the product into the sales pitch. And the designer needs systems thinking as a competency to translate the principles of "reduce, reuse, recycle", into designing. In general, it is expected that different skills and competencies will be needed to complete the anticipated transitions successfully. This will be covered in Chapter 10 about competencies.

Tipping points in different functions

There are various functions that are important to embed sustainability into an organization. In the book *Managing the Transition to a Sustainable Enterprise*[13], scientific evidence supports the selection of the following functional areas:

- Sales, marketing and brand
- Personnel, HR
- Finance and control
- IT
- Public affairs and corporate communications
- Procurement or purchasing
- Operations and QHSE (quality, health, safety and environment)
- Internal logistics and facilities

- General management and strategy
- R&D, product development and innovation.

These areas can provide an important stimulus to the integration of sustainability in the organization. As a Mentor, the CSO, CSR or sustainability manager has to support the translation of sustainability for each of these functional areas. Highlighting how sustainability creates value in each of these functions, strengthens and deepens that integration.

As a Mentor, you may want to start with those functional areas in which the value of sustainability is the most visible or tangible. This will vary with each company, of course, and is separate from (and on top of) the contribution every individual can make to the sustainability goals. For example, everyone can play a role in energy conservation and waste reduction by consistently switching off the lights and using less paper.

In addition, as a Mentor, you have to note and be capable of relating to every job level from the strategic to an operational level; each function has different job levels. For example, with the CFO, you talk about the introduction of new sustainable business models and with the financial controller, you discuss the quality of the sustainability metrics. With the HR director, you talk about strategic employee management and with the HR advisor, you discuss changing the company's "work-related mobility guidelines" to promote more sustainable behavior.

Sales, marketing and brand

Embedding sustainability in the marketing team and brand is an important step in the maturity model for the integration of sustainability in an organization. Marketers hold a key position at level 4 of the maturity model (Figure 4.2). When market research (by agencies trusted by the marketing team) and/or customer surveys show that clients will buy or pay more for sustainable products and services, you have a strong case to convince the marketing team. Be careful with the numbers though, you cannot take research results at face value, as people are likely to provide socially desirable answers that do not perfectly match their actual behavior in the future.

Janice Lao is Director, Group Corporate Responsibility and Sustainability at the Hongkong and Shanghai Hotels (HSH):

"Guests have different expectations of service now — they expect that as a luxury brand, we've already taken care of these issues. Guests want sustainable luxury: luxury without the negative impacts, which business activities can have on the environment and society."

But how do you convince marketers when customers are not asking for sustainable solutions, or are not willing to pay more? Forcing your own personal conviction upon them or trying to enforce the integration of sustainability through line management may actually work against what you are trying to achieve. To convince sales, marketing and brand, it is key to show that there are other ways sustainability can add value; for example, having a positive impact on corporate reputation and resilience in periods of negative or more critical news about the company. There are ways in which sustainability fuels the growth of the company other than an increase in sales or price.

Sometimes sustainability comes in a disguise and is translated into something the customer specifically desires, such as "cost savings" in the case of more energy-efficient appliances or the "convenience" of dry shampoo. As a CSO or CSR manager, it is therefore very effective to research the expectations clients have around sustainability, together with the marketing and sales teams. This enables you to translate sustainability to a relevant product innovation.

In addition, you can also gain the attention of marketing and sales by stimulating customers to demand more sustainable products and services. Especially in the business-to-business (B2B) environment, as CSO or CSR manager, you can influence demand by clients. For example, by staging an event where clients are updated about key initiatives and the state of sustainability in the industry.

Finally, integrating sustainability into your brand might be extremely relevant for companies that aim for purpose-driven consumers. Esther Verburg — Vice-President of Corporate Responsibility at Tommy Hilfiger Global/PVH Europe:

> *"Sustainability is about relevance and resilience. In order to stay relevant for today's purpose-driven consumer, integrating sustainability in your brand in an authentic way is a must. Due to the changing world around us, with dwindling resources and climate instability, making your value chain more sustainable is also a matter of building resilience and being able to cope with, and adapt, to that change."*

Personnel and HR

There are various ways in which sustainability can be made relevant for the HR team. It can contribute to the development of a social sustainability strategy, such as an inclusive society. In the Mentor role, the CSO or CSR manager works with HR to identify social aspects of sustainability, such as:

■ Diversity policy
■ Long-term vitality and employability of people
■ Opportunities for people with limited access to the labor market.

Moreover, sustainability is both a useful and smart instrument for human resource management:

■ Useful: sustainability leads to organizational engagement, employee satisfaction, motivated and inspired employees and lower staff turnover
■ Smart: it helps to attract and retain talent.

Building up knowledge on sustainability can take quite some time as HR usually has a more internal focus with less attention for social issues in society. In some organizations, HR has a greater role in societal engagement, through charity work, philanthropy and the management of Corporate Foundations.

Embedding sustainability in HR instruments can leverage a large part of generating support and creating sustainable success. Sustainability goals and behavior can be included in instruments such as:

■ Appraisals
■ Performance reviews
■ Codes of conduct
■ Training and introduction programs
■ Management development programs
■ Core values.

In the 2018 State of the Profession survey, Dutch CSOs, CSR and sustainability managers were asked to what degree sustainability was integrated in HR processes using the following questions:

■ Mentioned in all recruitment processes for the company?
■ Discussed during the on-boarding process for all employees?
■ Included in the job descriptions of all employees?
■ Included in performance reviews of all employees?
■ Considered during the job promotion process for all employees?
■ Included as a training and development opportunity for all employees?
■ Included in the personnel development goals of all employees?

Sustainability is primarily integrated in recruitment and on-boarding processes, and this partial embedment is again confirmed by the results of the 2019 survey. However, by fully embedding sustainability in HR processes, new and current employees immediately become more aware of the company's ambitions and the expectations for their own role and competencies regarding sustainability. HR is precisely the department to boost CSR from the bottom up, by hiring employees with important competencies needed for sustainability, such as collaboration and a strong feeling for integrity and system thinking (as discussed in Chapter 10). HR can also play an important role in helping the CSO or CSR manager develop support by creating common sustainability values, by involving people in being able to bear responsibility and by an open discussion, if behavior does deviate from the common value, defined in core values and/or codes of conduct.

Last but not least, next to embedding sustainability in formal instruments and development of new "sustainable competencies", HR staff might be actively involved in the informal organization of driving sustainability within the company. It is therefore very helpful to include HR in the formal organization of sustainability (such as the Council).

Finance and control

Embedding sustainability through the financial processes in the organization provides an important opportunity. The finance function can play a role, for example, in developing metrics for the sustainability objectives and KPIs, ensuring the data integrity of the gathered information, generating data for quarterly or yearly sustainability updates, the assessment of sustainability elements in investment proposals, budgets and by including sustainability data and achievements in the annual report. Especially in the reporting cycle, sustainability and finance can really strengthen each other. Chapter 8 on monitoring covers this in more detail. The finance area can add tremendous value by improving the sustainability data processes and — through those — the management, for better results.

Elfrieke van Galen (Co-Founder Sustainability University Foundation):

> *"Many finance professionals initially find sustainability a bit vague. Sustainability data is often less concrete than the financial data with which they are familiar. But that does not mean colleagues from finance cannot contribute to nonfinancial data."*

The finance team controls the annual budgeting process. In the budgeting or business planning process, general principles are shared throughout the organization. If sustainability is included as part of these principles or starting points and is also included in the strategic framework, then finance can supervise the inclusion of sustainability in the planning cycle, as well as in the quarterly and annual updates and meetings. When a company is just getting started with sustainability, this may not yet be included in the strategic framework.

Including sustainability in investment proposals also supports the integration of sustainability into the organization. To gradually increase the commitment, this is best done in a stepwise approach. A first step could be to assess investment proposals qualitatively on whether they have a positive or negative impact on the sustainability strategy. This usually leads to rich discussions, which can be very fruitful. A further step could be to quantify these effects and impacts. More detail on impact measurement is provided in Chapter 8.

The value of sustainability for finance varies in every company. It could be cost savings by energy and waste reduction, avoiding risk in the supply chain, creating a financially resilient future with more sustainable products and business, or the growing ESG transparency and the opportunities and risks that follow from the increased interest of investors and other stakeholders in sustainability information (Chapter 8).

Michael Kobori (former VP Sustainability at Levi Strauss & Co.) sees a need for the development of more financial skills of sustainability professionals:

"I have a strong view that sustainability professionals are not very familiar with finance and that has hindered their effectiveness. Sustainability professionals should be better educated in finance and also speak that language. To give an example from my experience: I have developed a strong partnership with finance because of supply chain financial risks, such as water and energy costs and opened up opportunities to work with financial institutions such as the World Bank (IFC) and VCs to finance innovation."

Sustainable investment strategies, like investment in renewable, climate-resilient or circular production facilities as well as implementing new sustainable business models, like "product as a service", require financial skills to at least understand their impact on the total financial portfolio and resilience of a company. A CSO or CSR manager really has to understand finance and relate to the CFO on a personal level to get support, because existing processes and criteria for (formats, rates of return) for board approval, are not suited to this type of "new" business investment. You really need to be creative and, for instance, first provide proof (with smaller pilots to find the data) to build your (financial) business case.

However, it also requires different skills and new ways of working from the finance department. For new business models, such as models based on circular economy, the finance department, which is based on linear financial accounting models for instance, has to find new ways of circular accounting and accepting new unknown risks.

Public Affairs and communications
Communications is a key functional area for embedding sustainability in the organization. Both external and internal communications can contribute to people becoming more aware of the sustainable choices they can take. Such positive messages also contribute to a more positive image of the company or product. This is where part of the business case for sustainability comes to life.

To convince the communications team to include sustainability topics in their communications channels, two approaches are particularly helpful:
■ Newsworthiness: package verifiable sustainability facts in such a way that they become newsworthy; for example, by highlighting that this is "the largest", "the first" or something with "tremendous impact"
■ Clear messaging: detailed and very nuanced stories are not usually effective nor engaging.

It is challenging to communicate continuously about sustainability. In part, this is due to regular, daily tasks and in part due to current events to which a company may have to respond. One way to resolve this is to use different communications channels, such as the "frequent touch point" locations of people during the day. That is, physical locations that are frequently visited or seen by clients or staff, such as the coffee area, the website or sales channels.

CSR and sustainability managers often get asked why they do not share sustainability credentials more frequently, even though a large part of their time is dedicated to working with the communications team to create sustainability campaigns. As with all communications campaigns, communicating sustainability is about repetition (as described in Chapter 5) and most companies could improve the storytelling around sustainability. You hardly ever hear or see the story behind the sustainability strategy. Storytelling is most powerful when you share the full story, including daring to be vulnerable, sharing dilemmas and things that did not go as well as planned.

In addition to communications, the public affairs team also plays an important role in the integration, due to its relationship with key stakeholders and its lobbying activities. Chapter 2 about the Network role, highlights the importance of proactively putting sustainability topics on the agenda in stakeholder dialogues. The public affairs team is both a key source of information for the sustainability manager as well as an important communications channel towards relevant stakeholders. In addition, public affairs can also add sustainability to the agenda of networks, organizations, parties, and committees which are relevant to fulfill the sustainability ambitions. This can include many different sustainability topics, such as emissions targets, packaging, labor conditions, fair-trade and tax policies.

Procurement

Procurement managers are mostly process or project managers in the procurement process. They can provide advice but, in the end, their internal customer (the business) decides. This is a key challenge for the integration of sustainability in procurement processes. Yet, the influence of procurement managers should not be underestimated as they know the market better than anyone else and are aware of potential sustainable alternatives. A proactive sustainability approach to procurement is a key opportunity for most companies. It can transform the procurement department into an innovation department. Therefore, this is a key team for the sustainability manager to Mentor and work with.

The value of sustainability for the procurement manager is, however, highly dependent on the relevance of sustainability for business and management. If the key and only indicator for procurement is cutting costs, you might want to team up with business first to let them specify their sustainable demands. Proactively minimizing reputational risks in the supply chain could be such a business demand, since the reputation of a company can be damaged if it becomes public that the manufacturing of its products is not sustainable, harming the environment or people.

Sustainable procurement is focused on a few key questions:
- What is the sustainability track record of the supplier (on sustainability topics relevant to your business)?
- How sustainable is the product or service at each stage in the life cycle?
  - Manufacturing (and previous steps in the supply chain, including mining)
  - Transportation to and from the place of use
  - Usage
  - Disposal.

To find out how sustainable a supplier is, you can use existing global evaluation tools and rating agencies, such as EcoVadis[14], that help procurement teams monitor the CSR or ESG (Environmental, Social and Governance) practices in the supply chains. It is important that the procurement team has relevant and up-to-date information about the suppliers: information that you might need in the Monitor role. All suppliers should comply with the applicable social and environmental laws and legislation, something that could be included in the general terms of procurement. For products with supply chains in high-risk countries, you will need to set up more elaborate processes; for example, through on-site audits. It might be quite a journey with the procurement team to address the above-mentioned questions. Fortunately, many tools have been developed in this field; for instance, by the Worldbank[15] and World Business Council for Sustainable Development (WBCSD).

Depending on the ambition of the company, as a Mentor, the CSO or CSR manager may work closely with procurement and suppliers, not only to minimize risk but also to create sustainable value. Embedding sustainability in the value chain is one of the steps a company goes through in the transitions towards sustainable value creation (Figure 3.5). To contribute to a circular economy, partnerships with suppliers in the value chain are crucial to building circular business systems. This requires the establishment of (longer-term) partnerships, which takes quite some time and effort to develop. Since sustainability is evolving, a longer-term partnership requires dynamic specification and you could, for instance, agree to a continuous increase of sustainable value during the partnership. For this, you have to define very precisely the sustainability goal that you want to achieve together, but you do not exactly define the road towards the goal. It takes very clear agreements on monitoring and steering the (output of the) partnership, since this creates more risks in contracts. Next to the interpersonal skills, as pointed out in the beginning of this chapter, long-term partnerships with suppliers requires "foresight thinking".

For companies with limited innovative capabilities, most sustainable innovations will have to come from the suppliers. The time required to find sustainable innovations in the market or to create innovative partnerships is often limited. It can therefore be very helpful to proactively — together with procurement — find out which type of product or services need to be purchased or even be co-developed during the coming year(s), so that you can anticipate and create more time.

The Pareto principle often applies and, with ten to twenty large projects, you can probably impact 80% of the purchasing volume. Start by listing the ten largest procurement processes in your organization based on materiality and impact. If you set up meetings with the managers of each of these processes to investigate the potential sustainability improvements, you have probably made very large strides in the integration. Of course, this will require the involvement of the internal owners or budget holders, as they will ultimately need to approve the ideas generated.

Nowadays, many suppliers also have a sustainability strategy. This might create opportunities; for instance, by organizing meetings with suppliers to identify mutual interests and sustainable innovations without extra costs. In this case, the CSO combines the Networker, Mentor and Innovator role.

IT

Although IT can be seen as part of operations and/or part of procurement, it has evolved as such a key strategic enabler across companies, that sustainability and CSR managers need to think more holistically about how the IT department can support enterprise-wide corporate sustainability efforts.

On one hand, IT infrastructure such as computers and servers and IT-related activities are a significant source of energy use, greenhouse gas emissions and have a social impact. This is especially so when every stage of its production and use life cycle is accounted for, such as manufacturing (including mining), transportation, use and disposal. In addition, computers generate heat and it often takes as much energy to cool computing equipment as it takes to run it. Making IT infrastructure and IT-related activities more sustainable and efficient in the company itself or in the supply chain can have a great impact on saving costs, lowering greenhouse gas emissions and improving labor conditions.

On the other hand, IT can be a successful enabler in reaching the corporate sustainability goals; for instance, with smart energy-saving software or more innovative applications such as machine learning (as described in Chapter 7 on the Innovator role).

Operations and QSHE

In the context of this chapter, the term "operations" refers to the core manufacturing process, the way in which input is transformed to output in the most efficient way.

The operational or manufacturing process is an important lever to create sustainable success and to become a sustainable company. In most organizations, there are many opportunities to reduce both use of resources and waste; for example, through energy efficiency and waste-management programs. Often, some programs for this are already in place. In that case, it is vital to engage with such initiatives in order to connect and strengthen them. The cost savings generated by this waste reduction are an important part of the business case for sustainability. More importantly, a tipping point is created when sustainability is integrated in the core manufacturing process: not only from the perspective of efficiency improvements, cost reductions and compliance but also to support the credibility and reputation of the organization in its sustainability communications.

As employees in the manufacturing process usually have useful ideas about opportunities for improvement, the Mentor role should be a facilitating role, leaving the generation of plans to the craftspeople on the work floor. Workshops are one way of doing this, with the sustainability team providing guidance. If this is done in the same way, as other strategic goals of the strategic framework are shared with the manufacturing team, it will become clear that sustainability is not just an "add-on", but really part of the core of the business. Once sustainable practices have been developed, they can be integrated in training or other company learning tools.

Depending on the type of company, there could also be a QSHE team or manager, looking after quality, environment, safety and health and compliance with relevant regulations in those fields. Systemic environmental management is focused on creating systems and processes needed to continuously improve the environmental performance. The objective is to effectively manage those activities that have an impact on the environment and to reduce that impact. ISO 14001 could be a relevant tool to use. If such an environmental management system is not yet in place, establishing one can be a way to continuously improve the environmental performance. Certification may not be required, but it can be an effective way to demonstrate to clients (in the B2B market) or suppliers that your company is taking its environmental impact seriously.

(Internal) logistics

Logistics is an area in which sustainability is very much aligned with the operational objectives, but it is also an area where the word sustainability is not used very frequently. The logistics department plans and organizes the flow of goods through an organization. Depending on the company, this department also includes stock management and transportation. Critical success factors include speed, reliability and the lowest costs possible. This can be achieved by completely filling up trucks and by planning their routes as efficiently as possible. This, of course, aligns very well with a sustainability-related goal around the reduction of emissions.

Logistics is often outsourced, so you might end up dealing with a contract manager in charge of handling the logistics contracts. In the Mentor role, it is important to work with logistics in order to have them — and procurement — integrate sustainability criteria into their procurement processes. This might include things like an assessment of the sustainability program and certifications of the logistics service provider or the use of alternative, more sustainable methods of transportation.

Just like other suppliers, logistics companies can contribute to achieving sustainability goals. Engaging them actively with the sustainability goals and plans, rather than just asking them to execute a plan in which they have no role, will be more likely to generate useful ideas from them.

The way in which you use and order goods in your own organization also has a direct effect on the logistics side of your sustainability plan. For example, if you order office supplies every day, there will be daily deliveries. But by setting up a small stock of supplies in the office and only ordering once a month, the number of deliveries is reduced to just once a month as well.

Facilities is one of the supporting departments that can really make a difference in implementation of sustainability and in very visible parts of the company. Facility management manages, simply put, the household of a company, so that every staff member has all the services and resources (facilities) at his or her disposal to be able to do the job well, such as reception, catering, cleaning, heating, office equipment, supplies, furniture, coffee, waste management, real estate (management), building maintenance, security, mobility, parking facilities and so on. For a CSO or CSR manager is it crucial to cooperate with facilities to embed sustainability in every supporting process. Most of the ideas from employees about making the company more sustainable relate to facility processes, such as the use of coffee cups or fair-trade coffee, reducing plastic waste in the canteen, reusing office equipment, sharing initiatives like books, the sharing or introduction of company bikes. It is an opportunity for a CSO or CSR manager to use these often small-impact but very visible innovations, to engage employees and to show that the company is serious in its sustainability ambitions. On the contrary, if sustainability is not embedded in facilities, you might be confronted with unpleasant surprises. An example is the distribution of plastic water bottles instead of tap water at a company's event or little single-use plastic forks at an event about reducing single-use plastic waste!

Other functions

Embedding sustainability in other functional areas like general management and strategy as well as R&D, product development and innovation is covered in the chapters on the Strategist (Chapter 3) and the Innovator (Chapter 7).

6.2 **Mentoring in practice**

How do you introduce sustainability to the daily lives of your colleagues to make your organization more sustainable? Printing less and switching off the lights does not really make your company more sustainable in its core. Many employees understand quite well where the opportunities to improve lie, based on their craftsmanship and (in some cases) from their education. If your colleagues also experience sustainability as a natural part of their specific role, you have succeeded and generated broad support.

At NS, the sustainability department has developed a workshop to make sustainability relevant to different people. This voluntary workshop enables people to translate sustainability to their own role and area of expertise. Before coming to the workshop, participants are asked to calculate their own environmental footprint.[16] This provides insight into their own sustainability performance. Sharing the footprint scores with the group creates a positive sense of competition. People either want to do better or feel they can reapply their personal efforts at work.

After a more general presentation on sustainability and the NS sustainability strategy, the workshop continues with exploring the functional areas of the participants and dividing these into specific activities. For each activity, we brainstorm how to make it more sustainable or how it can contribute to making NS a more sustainable company. In these workshops, we also share how each team is already contributing to the sustainability strategy, with specific cases and projects. People are often surprised at what is in place already, even in their own team. At the end of the workshop, concrete actions are agreed upon and ownership allocated to the participants of the workshop. Often, the list of action includes a follow-up workshop to share the cases and projects with other colleagues within their functional area.
Another way of taking up your Mentor role is to publish cases and information on the intranet, LinkedIn or other social media. You can share current projects, include interactive elements such as quizzes, e-learning tools, a forum and tips per functional area, such as the poster we created across all teams (Figure 6.2).

It is also important to make the sustainability team very accessible, by making clear who is in the team and how they can be reached. Make sure people feel they are welcome to consult the sustainability team. You may want to establish consultation hours to make this a bit more manageable.

FIGURE 6.2 **Examples of possible sustainable actions per NS department (non-exhaustive list)**

Staff	
HR	1 Include sustainability in recruitment process and job description, either as a core criterion or in a more indirect way, by asking about the applicant's attitude towards sustainability. 2 Through both recruitment and promotion from within, increase diversity in the NS staff (women, different backgrounds, younger generations, special talents). 3 Include sustainability in the forms used for appraisals and performance reviews. 4 Integrate sustainability into the training program and/or offer a separate sustainable business module.
Communications	1 Communicate the sustainable characteristics of products and company (both internally and externally) to increase engagement and taking pride in NS for both clients and staff. 2 Take sustainability into account when planning communications tools and channels. For example, consider potential waste and materials usage of paper brochures. 3 Tell clients that they can contribute to a better environment by taking the train in off-peak hours or by separating their trash.
Press engagement	1 Know the sustainability facts and figures to be able to readily inform the press. 2 Always share with journalists how much more sustainable trains are versus cars. 3 Pro-actively share NS's sustainability activities and achievements for positive press coverage.
Procurement	1 Select suppliers on their sustainability merits and their ability to contribute to the sustainability strategy of NS. 2 Specify the required products or services in such a way that sustainability criteria must be taken into consideration in the selection process (material usage, energy efficiency, labor conditions). 3 Ask suppliers, including existing ones, to suggest sustainable alternatives or to contribute to sustainable innovations. 4 Discuss sustainability as a core criterion with the business.
Marketing	1 Map the perception and importance of sustainability among customers. 2 Leverage sustainability as a unique selling point of trains. 3 Obtain new customers by including sustainability in consumer marketing. 4 Guide travelers to use trains in off-peak hours to advance a more efficient use of the trains.
Business Development	1 Map the stakeholders and organize conversations to see if NS is still serving the stakeholders' needs. 2 Participate in thinking about sustainable business models (like circular economy). 3 Map the clients' wishes regarding the sustainability of our products and incorporate these in product innovation. 4 Optimize matching of supply and demand for mobility, making public transport more accessible and a better alternative for using a car.

Strategy	1 Take social issues and trends into account in the matching of long-term vision. 2 Benchmark/compare sustainability at NS with the competition and use their best practices to develop a sustainable strategy. 3 Organize dialogues to see if the NS strategy is still serving the stakeholders' needs. 4 Map the social value of NS and how it can be increased.
IT	1 Use and install energy-efficient hardware and components, produced with efficient use of materials, which are recycled at the end of their life cycle. 2 Provide efficient server usage by using virtualization, for example. 3 Support paperless IT and more efficient flexible offices and work processes.
Legal	1 Adopt sustainability arrangements in supplier contracts. 2 Advise on national and European laws and regulations regarding sustainable and social aspects (including privacy and ethics) with which NS should comply, reducing the risk of violating these laws and regulations. 3 Support specific new developments in regards to sustainability in intellectual ownership or privacy, for instance.
Finance	1 Deliver transparent reporting about sustainability performances, according to GRI or other relevant guidelines and have them checked by the accountant. 2 Check if all investment proposals have a section on the impact on the environment. 3 Deliver quarterly reports on sustainability performances and advise management on adjustments. 4 Research all subsidy possibilities for sustainable development and advise the (project) managers about them.

Management & Support

Management (general)	1 Discuss with the team what its contribution can be to the sustainable strategy of NS. 2 Make this discussion a part of your regular work meeting, target letter or assessment interviews. 3 Lead by example regarding sustainability. 4 Ask decision-makers about the sustainability aspects of the investment proposals and projects. 5 Make sure that sustainability is part of the curriculum when choosing education and training for the employees.
Operational management	1 Take (e-)courses about driving energy-efficient and working sustainable, giving you insight into what your team can contribute to a more sustainable NS. 2 Make sustainability a part of the regular work meeting or assessment interview. 3 Support energy-efficient driving to make sure that the targets are reached. Communicate the performances in the canteens. 4 Be an example by: turning off the lights in empty rooms, separating your waste, etc.
Retail management	1 Frequently discuss what can be done in the shops' assortments and interiors to increase sustainability. 2 See that energy-efficient equipment is purchased and minimize the loss of heat and coolness in shops. 3 Think about minimizing waste in shops by using less or different packaging or returning packaging to the supplier. 4 Store more organic and fair-trade products in the shops.

Secretaries and assistants	1 Minimize the use of paper and take a course in working paperless (share best practices with your colleagues). 2 When booking an external location, take into account if it is accessible by public transport. 3 Support your manager or department in new ways of sustainable working. 4 When ordering lunch or catering, ask for organic alternatives, avoid single-use plastics.

Operations, service and retail

Train drivers	1 Do you like energy-efficient driving? Suggest to your colleagues to do it too. 2 If possible, put your train on stand-by modus at the end of the day. 3 If you can operate the heating, air-conditioning and lights, try to do this as energy-efficiently as possible. 4 Discuss ideas to become more sustainable with your colleagues and team manager.
Conductors	1 Help the train to drive economically by signaling for departure exactly on time. 2 When not in use, turn off the reading lights in the train. 3 On occasion, tell the customers/travelers how environmentally friendly the train is in comparison to the car. 4 Discuss ideas to become more sustainable with your colleagues and team manager.
Retail employees	1 Know which products in the assortment are organic and healthy in order to inform the customer. 2 Separate the waste of the store or return packaging back to the supplier. 3 Suggest to your manager what can be done more sustainably in the store. 4 Ask your customers if they desire a more sustainable assortment.
Service employees	1 On occasion, tell the customers/travelers how environmentally friendly the train is in comparison to the car. 2 When ordering paper or brochures, be as economical as you can. 3 Support travelers to board their train on time, helping the train driver and conductor to depart exactly on time, making energy-efficient driving possible. 4 Provide excellent services, because that is very important in convincing more people to travel by train. Someone taking the train and not using the car is traveling without CO_2.

Logistics & Information

Logistics	1 Support a more energy-efficient way train system by using energy-efficient trains, a time table design that has space for energy-efficient driving, energy-efficient infrastructure, the implementation of software and tools to support energy-efficient driving, etc. 2 Increase the occupancy rate in off-peak hours by better matching the number of trains with the number of travelers. 3 Logistical decisions are often based on a complex number of different arguments: can you map the priorities and use them to choose the most energy-efficient trains?
Information	1 Integrate the CO_2 comparison device in the travel app, showing the customer exactly how sustainable his/her mode of transportation is. 2 Develop travel information, including sustainable first and last mile options, to make public transport more attractive for travelers and make them leave their cars. 3 Support dispersion of travelers from rush hour to off-peak hours by showing a crowd indication in the travel app.

Real Estate & Facilities		
Facilities	1	When purchasing or ordering facility services, you can take many sustainability aspects into account: waste, use of heat, sensor-controlled light switches, energy-efficient devices, use of environmentally friendly cleaning products, organic assortment in the company restaurant, etc.
	2	During construction work, install sustainable devices: light sensors, water sensors, separate waste bins, insulation, more efficient installations, etc.
	3	Facilities also involves logistics: schedule these as efficient as possible to prevent unnecessary transport.
	4	Stimulate everyone who uses the company buildings to adopt more sustainable behavior.
Real estate (development)	1	Investigate the sustainability aspects of construction, like Breeam.
	2	On a scale of 1-10, determine how sustainable the NS is doing in construction right now and think how this can be improved.
	3	Ensure that renovations always lead to a better energy rating of the building.
	4	Advise about sustainable (circular) construction and investigate the real costs of sustainable building, it is not necessarily more expensive.
Real estate (maintenance)	1	Replace parts with more sustainable parts and lights with LED lights.
	2	Maintain installations and building regularly, using the full technical lifetime.
	3	Minimize energy use and use of materials in maintenance, schedule activities and transport as efficiently as possible.
	4	Propose measures to reduce energy and water usage in the buildings.
Maintenance & Service materials		
Train/material managers	1	Ensure that train materials are eligible for reuse at the end of their useful life.
	2	Specify or design new trains to make sure they have a long lifetime with minimal impact and can be "modernized" in a circular way when they are out of date.
	3	Enable separating waste in the train, use the climate system efficiently, use LED lighting, install water-efficient toilets without chemicals.
	4	Create zones for working and meeting in the trains and increase the accessibility of the trains.
Project management		
Project managers	1	In all projects, incorporate changes that contribute to the sustainable goals of NS in terms of being a climate-neutral and circular company and being a social and inclusive employer.
	2	Incorporate the sustainability impact of a project in investment proposals and project planning, displaying their impact as SMART as possible.
	3	Provide a socially responsible alternative business case to every regular business case and take social impact into account in the decision-making process.

6.3 The learning Mentor

Deployment of capacity

Within NS, many steps can still be taken with the promotion of CSR or sustainability to the workplace. Really actively recruiting and recommending is necessary to promote the workshops, which asks a great deal of capacity. There are still relatively few workshops conducted internally, although there is an internal sustainability platform providing much information. However, it is not visited and read frequently enough. There are still people who think that CSR or sustainability is not part of their job, since there is a sustainability team. If these people are in management positions, it is difficult to put that department in the saddle properly. Then you have to start with the manager. This also requires the deployment of capacity to start the conversation, to gain insight into the background of the resistance and to reverse it.

Can't know it all

You can ensure the inclusion of sustainability criteria in procurement by integrating it into each step of the procurement process. At NS, the sustainability team worked with procurement to establish and integrate relevant sustainability criteria at each step along the way. Figure 6.3 shows how the sustainability and procurement teams collaborate on this.

Although this is a great process, it is a challenge to include the right sustainability specifications in the tender plan. Procuring different products and services in different markets asks for creative and new sustainability specifications for suppliers and their products and services. Fortunately, much has

FIGURE 6.3 **NS sustainable procurement process**

- The request for information states that the contractor will have to adhere to the NS Supplier Code of Conduct
- The requests for information and proposal include a clause that the contractor will have to undergo an EcoVadis assessment and that an improvement plan will have to be developed if they score below 55

- Procurement manager and sustainability team explore the possibilities
- Procurement manager explores the possibilities with the business owner: if needed, the sustainability team can facilitate
- General sustainable procurement criteria are used for guidance

4
Request for information and proposal

1
Exploration

3
Tender board check

2
Tender plan

- The tender board checks the tender plan for inclusion of sustainable procurement criteria and whether the sustainability team has been consulted
- General sustainable procurement criteria are used for guidance

- Procurement manager integrates sustainable procurement criteria into the tender process, based on the conversations with the business owner and the sustainability team
- General sustainable procurement criteria are used for guidance

been learned over the years, and sustainability or CSR managers can benefit by learning from their peers how to find the most suitable specifications: frontrunner companies are often the first ones to come up with sustainable specifications. Next to the wind power for trains project, a good example is the procurement of the trains themselves. That process often starts more than five years in advance and trains also continue to run for decades. In order to make the correct sustainability specifications, you must therefore know very well what the long-term developments are in several areas, such as waste separation. Which waste streams will remain? Will there be so much paper in five years' time? Which icons will customers recognize? If it is still very unpredictable or unknown, the only option is to specify as much flexibility as possible, so that you can still adjust during use. And accept that you cannot know everything in advance.

6.4 The successful Mentor

It takes time and in-depth knowledge of the business to be a successful Mentor, but it can be a tipping point in embedding sustainability in an organization.

Esther Verburg — Vice-President of Corporate Responsibility at Tommy Hilfiger Global/PVH Europe explains how:

> *"In the Mentor role you use the in-depth knowledge of the business to translate the overall sustainability strategy to (local) targets and actions for several business functions. Doing this in a co-creational manner creates essential ownership within the business. By involving different functions across the organization from VP level to young professionals — next to boardroom support — we created a tipping point in the maturity of sustainability in our company."*

This is how she engaged brand management and procurement in her Mentor role.

Sales, marketing and brand management

Brand management is crucial to accelerate the integration of sustainability in the business, especially when it is a consumer-facing business. As Simon Sinek (Chapter 3) explains, those companies that know very well why they exist are the ones to inspire and attract clients and talent. Integrating your sustainability and your brand strategy results in one clear "why" in communications externally and internally. It becomes clear that sustainability is an inseparable part of the business strategy, as the message is taken up in every relevant business communication, rather than being brought as a separate message.

Esther Verburg explains that once the sustainable strategy was shaped from a brand perspective and linked to the brand strategy in 2018, all pieces came together. The brand purpose and sustainability strategy were interlinked and founded on the heritage of the brand, and the "why" of the company was reflected in the brand strategy. It incorporates the same determined optimism of the founder, who knew where he wanted to go when he started his business, selling jeans from the trunk of his car and, although he did not exactly know how to get there, was determined not to give up on his vision. This value also fueled the sustainable strategy. Co-creation with the Brand Strategy team and Chief Brand officer resulted in sustainability being brought into the heart of the brand, and the business is now driving sustainability forward through initiatives like jeans made from 100% recycled cotton and an adaptive wear line for people with disabilities. Sustainability already had a value for the company but now it also creates value for the brand.

Procurement

The Mentor role of a CSO or CSR manager in procurement can be intensive, as it needs a good deal of research and training if you want to involve the entire supply chain. The first step is to find out what and where the impacts are, what is material and what is in your stakeholder's and company's interest?

Esther Verburg:

"Nowadays, in the fashion industry, it is largely known where the impacts are. For instance, cotton has a very big impact, both environmentally and socially. The supply chain of cotton is so complex that you can only decrease the negative impact if you work together with other parties like peer brands and retailers, NGOs, and the so-called multi-stakeholder initiatives like, for example, the Better Cotton Initiative. Once you have set procurement targets, you have to find out who makes decisions about what's in the supply chain and who is responsible. Then you bring on board everyone who is relevant, such as sourcing teams, product developers, garment vendors and fabric mills, often providing training in the process.

It takes a lot of effort to make this a 'business as usual' process. We had to learn how this really worked in the beginning, but then the adoption pace of more sustainable cotton in our supply chain picked up quickly and we hope to reach our goal of 100% more sustainable cotton in 2020."

The example of another supply chain gives you an idea of the complexity: if you want to source sustainable milk, you have to know what the cow eats, what nutrients are put in that food, the vet responsible for the health of the animal, where it sleeps, how the milk is collected, by whom, how it is transported and so on. A variety of companies and individuals are part of a production process and you have to involve all of them. Because of this complexity, collaboration across the value chain is important and multi-stakeholder initiatives can often bring benefits such as:

1   Collective resources
2   Same requirements for the supply chain
3   Covering all (complex) parts of the supply chain.

Renewable energy — wind for the trains — Mentor role

Sustainability in sales & marketing
When preparing for the procurement of renewable energy, a financial framework was developed. What price is acceptable, taking into account that renewable energy had added value for our stakeholders and customers but should not increase the price of a train ticket? The commercial department was asked to calculate the potential for growth in the number of journeys made if all train journeys were without CO_2 emissions. This insight involved the commercial department and made it clear that it is an important purchasing criterion for a large part of the customers. Ensuring the sustainability of the commercial proposition is a development that started back then, at the creation of the financial framework and that is increasing every year, both towards consumers and business customers. Successful results have been achieved with the Low Car Diet for several years: a competition between companies to make the least "fossil (car) kilometers", through smart use of public transport, bicycle, car sharing or by traveling less. This appears to be an effective and easily accessible way of making companies and employees aware of the possibilities and benefits of a consciously sustainable choice of transport. Low Car Diet was co-launched with Urgenda, the NGO famous for winning a historic climate lawsuit. With the same behavioral science insights, a program has recently been

LOWCARDIET
POWERED BY FYNCH

developed for the business client, focusing on internal competition and behavioral change instead of competition with other companies.

The proposition of a climate-neutral train journey nowadays (2019) is a key selling point in marketing, both towards consumer and business customers. It is not the most important one, but account managers increasingly include it in their sales pitch. Due to the 2015 Paris Climate Treaty, climate-neutral travel has become more important, especially with business clients looking for ways to reduce their carbon footprint. At the start of the Paris Treaty, Corporate Mobility Pledges with fifteen companies were made to reduce the carbon footprints of business-related mobility by 50%. This has evolved into a Community of (best) Practice "Smart Travelling", with about fifty of the biggest Dutch companies. They have developed and implemented a set of best practices to reach their goals. One of the best practices is to travel by climate-friendly train instead of car or plane. As shown in Figure 6.4, other environmentally friendly means of transport in the Netherlands can also contribute significantly to these goals.

FIGURE 6.4 **CO_2 emissions (grams per traveler per kilometer) from cars, trains, and bikes in the Netherlands**

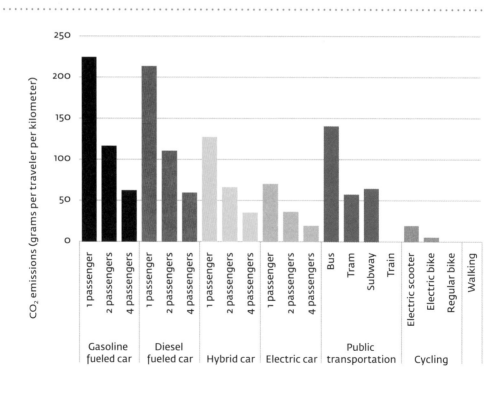

FIGURE 6.5 **The Green Train**

Sustainability in communications

Key consumer touch points for NS are the trains themselves. To remind people that the train is the most sustainable method of transportation and that it runs on renewable wind energy, one train was redecorated green on the outside. For the design of this Green Train, NS ran a competition, which gave further publicity to the topic (Figure 6.5).

From the start of the project, the communication department was involved and convinced of the value of communicating information about the wind-powered trains. Next to regular campaigns, the Green Train was one of the other means of communication. However it was not until 2017, when all trains were running on 100% wind power and the current CEO wanted to share this great news with the rest of the world, that the communication department found a way that really reached out. This is described in Chapter 7, in the discussion on the Innovator role.

Tips for Mentors

- Analyze the business processes to determine which sustainable changes have to be made in functions, activities and tasks.
- Per function, show how sustainability can enrich it.
- Provide concrete examples of how sustainability has been translated for that department in other companies or organizations.
- Let people define for themselves how they can contribute in their own role; for example, through workshops.
- If you develop a process of co-creation with a wide circle of your internal stakeholders, you will dig up the in-depth knowledge necessary to operationalize and embed your policy. In the process, you create business ownership and this gives a boost to the maturity level of sustainability: crucial in making the transition to a sustainable business.
- Make sustainability personal, for example, by having people calculate their own environmental footprint.
- Every type of motivation is good, as long as it leads to more sustainable behavior.
- Make it fun!
- Consider how sustainability can help the other person grow.
- Leverage the power of storytelling: personal struggles and dilemmas inspire more than technical guides.
- Use a structured and project-driven approach to increase your effectiveness.
- Invest in growing your own knowledge about the functional area and language of the target audience.
- Linking sustainability to your brand strategy will lead to the sustainability agenda becoming one with the business agenda. This will anchor ownership and drive forward sustainability in the organization, accelerating progress.
- It is OK to say you do not know the answer either.
- Be creative. When people say things are impossible, ask "what is possible?".
- Ask many questions and do not make any assumptions. Some things are that way just because they have been that way for years.
- Be patient. If something does not work out immediately, come back to it later. Start where things are easier and turn those projects into success stories.
- Do not depend on just one person in each team, but broaden the engagement.
- Let people share the story with each other, in the language of their own profession.
- Keep communicating and sharing the successes to increase engagement and participation in workshops and e-learning.
- Make sure people feel they are welcome to consult the sustainability team.

The Innovator

*"The people who are crazy enough to think they
can change the world are the ones who do."*

STEVE JOBS (1955-2011), CO-FOUNDER AND FORMER CEO OF APPLE

A CSO, CSR or sustainability manager has an important role in fueling innovation. As an Innovator, the CSO challenges others and him/herself to "innovate" for sustainable development. (S)he shows leadership and courage and is able to find and develop sustainable innovations with impact, by combining a cross-functional way of working with external orientation. Partnerships within the value chain are a key source of innovation, but there are sources outside the value chain as well. For example, Google issued open calls to organizations around the world to submit their ideas on how they could use artificial intelligence (AI) to help address societal challenges.

To be an "outside-the-box" and "step-changing" Innovator, the Innovator needs the trust of the organization. It is more likely to see a substantial Innovator role for CSOs in organizations that have already embedded sustainability and/or for CSOs who have worked in their organization for quite some time.

An important activity in the Innovator role is to embed sustainability in the innovations process in such a way that all innovations are sustainable or lead to sustainability-related improvements. In companies without a strong innovation culture, the Innovator role consists of initiating an innovation process, or so-called "funnel for sustainable innovations". The challenge for the CSO in that situation is knowing what to prioritize and to find business owners for the ideas or innovations in the funnel.

As an Innovator, a CSO should be aware of innovation trends and their possibilities and impacts.

"A CSO should be aware of disruptive technologies such as blockchain, virtual reality, machine learning, quantum computers. In his/her Innovator role, a CSO should proactively introduce these technologies to obtain UN Global Goals faster and might also engage employees by stimulating them to develop technologies for certain needs of society, such as wildfire (prevention) technologies."

DARLENE DAMM (CHAIR AND PRINCIPAL FACULTY OF GLOBAL
GRAND CHALLENGES AT SINGULARITY UNIVERSITY)

This chapter explains the relevance of the Innovator role for the CSO and showcases examples of how to be an effective Innovator. How the introduction of new "disruptive" technologies might affect the role of the CSO — like focusing on more ethical questions — is discussed in the chapter about sustainability dynamics.

7.1 Sustainable innovation processes

The impact of effective CSOs in their Innovator role can be crucial for the transition to a sustainable world. Innovation teams are driving future products, operations and, therefore, future business models. By embedding sustainability in innovation and/or design teams, business will develop in a profitable and sustainable way, based on the needs of society.

For companies with a sustainable strategy that see sustainability as an opportunity for growth, sustainability is usually deeply embedded in the development of new products and business models. For companies with ambitious sustainability goals, incremental approaches are insufficient. The Innovator needs to drive innovative breakthroughs or systemic change to live up to the ambitions.

For companies at the start of their sustainability journey, the CSO, CSR or sustainability manager will have to join up with existing projects and processes to ensure innovations deliver sustainable outcomes or are seen as sustainability projects. This is closely related to the Mentor role (Chapter 6), translating sustainability for the innovations team.

In short, CSOs, CSR and sustainability managers can stimulate sustainable innovation in two ways:

1   Make every innovation more sustainable
2   Driving sustainable innovations.

Making innovation more sustainable

Making every innovation sustainable begins by making sustainability the starting point for the selection of ideas in the innovation process. The innovation process can take many forms, such as an idea-management system, a project board or the governance of an innovation fund. Whatever the structure of the innovation process in your company, you can integrate sustainability into the selection criteria and templates for innovation.

For companies with a clear innovation funnel with distinct steps and filters, the CSO, CSR or sustainability manager can embed sustainability criteria in every selection step along the way (Figure 7.1). Of the many ideas generated, ideas which score well on sustainability (and other) criteria can be progressed to the next step in which an idea is turned into a design. Of all the designs, only those that score high on sustainability can progress to the analysis phase. When the analysis shows that the expected sustainability results can be achieved, a well-substantiated action plan can be developed.

The weighting of sustainability in the different stages is determined in collaboration with the innovation manager. Sustainability can be a minimum

FIGURE 7.1 **Example of an innovation funnel with filters**

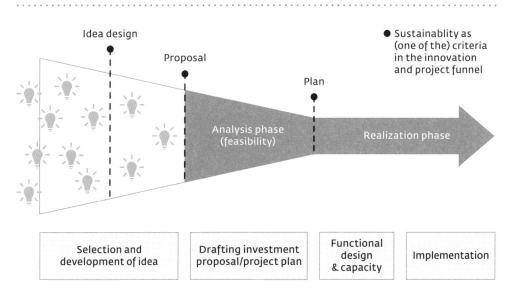

129

requirement, one of many criteria, or the most important criterion. For example, if CO_2 reduction is a key target, only those ideas and projects that lead to a significant reduction in CO_2 will make it through the funnel.

Sustainability criteria can also play a role in other innovation processes, such as "idea" competitions. For internal idea-generation processes, nowadays a substantial part of ideas include a sustainability element or serve a sustainability goal.

When such a structured innovation process is not in place, your task as an Innovator is to determine how you can make every innovation sustainable. There are three ways to do this:

1 Investigate how and where innovations come about in the company
2 Consider how sustainability can be used as a starting point
3 Integrate sustainability into implementation plans for innovations.

Driving sustainable innovations

Sustainable innovations are generated only when those innovations that result in (more) sustainable products and services are stimulated and selected. Again, as the Innovator, the CSR manager has to find out whether the company has an innovation process or not. If such a process is in place, making products and services more sustainable can be set as a target. By only progressing sustainable innovations through the funnel, the sustainable product portfolio will grow over time.

If no such process exists or if it is insufficient to meet your goals, as CSO, CSR or sustainability manager, you can initiate one; for example, by organizing an internal idea-generation contest. Do ensure there are sponsors within the organization to support these ideas with money and other resources. Another example could be establishing an external innovation fund, crowdsourcing initiatives or open calls to suppliers. Such initiatives really fuel the innovation power within and outside the company.

There seems to be a real difference between making innovations more sustainable and driving sustainable innovations but, in reality, there is quite a mix of both. As innovation is a process that requires openness and collaboration, it is often less clearly structured. As the Innovator, the CSR or CSO manager will, therefore, have to be flexible and apply different approaches and interventions. To be effective, the Innovator will need quite some intuition and entrepreneurship. This could require initiating a project you really believe in without the buy-in of the organization. Selecting and supporting winning ideas is a crucial part of the art of innovation. This includes the acceptance of failures and learning from them!

Initiating innovation

There are many ways to structure the innovation process and a myriad of theories and definitions about innovation. For the Innovator, is it key to know what is in place and to assess whether this will deliver the innovations needed to achieve the sustainability goals or strategy and — if that is not the case — how to bridge the gap.

With this portfolio assessment of different kinds of innovation projects, McKinsey's three horizon model[17] (Figure 7.2) can help. It differentiates the following kind of innovation projects:

- Innovations within the existing organization and with external parties focused on the first and second horizon; i.e., focused on making current products more efficient and renewing the product offer
- External innovations focused on the third horizon, or rather the creation of new products and services as well as sustainable business models.

Whether the three horizons are still bound by time can by argued with the current development of disruptive technologies. However, the different type of focus of the innovations still holds.

FIGURE 7.2 **McKinsey's Three Horizon Model**

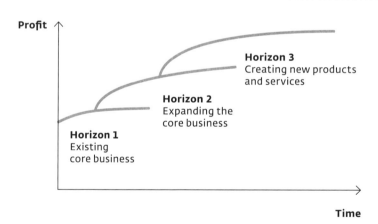

Horizons 1 and 2: optimization and renewal

When using internal capacity for sustainable innovations, the Innovator role overlaps with the Mentor role (Chapter 6). The Innovator role also over-laps with the Stimulator role (Chapter 5), which targets incremental renewal within different departments.

First and second horizon innovations are often generated by employees and are usually integrated into the corporate or project plans of the current organization. A key role for the Innovator for these types of innovations is to create an open environment where ideas can flourish and be implemented. This can include shielding people with innovative ideas from overly critical people and from endless administrative procedures and by connecting them to relevant sponsors within the company.

It is very likely that the sustainability team regularly receives ideas and improvements from other teams with the request to provide comments and tips. Be sure to leave the ownership of the idea with the Initiator, but you may want to offer support and guidance in taking the idea further. This could take several forms, such as highlighting the idea higher up in the organization (escalation), creating connections with people or knowledge outside of the organization or freeing up (temporary) capacity or funds.

To spark the sustainability element of such innovations, it is helpful to have a sense of urgency for sustainable change within the organization. In the Stimulator role, the CSR or CSO manager has an important influence on this sense of urgency.

Stakeholders

Stakeholders are a fantastic source of inspiration and innovation. You can use their (external) capacities to create sustainable improvements. As CSO or CSR manager, you are then both the Innovator and the Networker (Chapter 2). Stakeholders can be engaged to renew or optimize the product portfolio; for example, through co-creation. Such innovation journeys often take place with suppliers. Mostly, such co-creation journeys are aimed at the first and second horizons, targeting expansion or further development of existing activities or products.

Horizon 3: creating new products and services

For large companies, innovation on the third horizon independently is a challenge. This is caused by the increasing complexity of the external surroundings and the risk-averse, usually quite bureaucratic structures, of large companies.

Creating an innovation ecosystem such as an investment fund outside the organization can then be an effective way forward. The French Railways (SCNF) set up such an investment fund with the objective of generating and developing sustainable renewal ideas. This was mostly focused on new products and services at the edge of their own systems. They could innovate outside of the limitations of their own company by investing money (venture capital) or resources (knowledge, network) in start-up ventures with relevant third horizon innovations. These companies and their people are much better at such innovations, due to their entrepreneurial approach.

The impact of "small" visible innovations

Type of projects that are more "ad hoc" innovations and are really more related to embedding sustainability in the organization tend to belong primarily to the Coordinator & Initiator role of the CSO, CSR or sustainability manager (Chapter 4) and not to the Innovator role. Through the initiation of these iconic or pilot projects, sustainability becomes more visible and they offer the opportunity to communicate tangible results. However, as the Innovator, it can also be of great value to keep an eye out for innovations and other achievements that really appeal to the imagination. These create their own newsworthiness, even if their potential impact is limited: smaller, visible experience innovations vouch for the sustainable nature of the company or product. It is crucial to include some of these types of innovation in your portfolio.

Figure 7.3 shows that innovations can have two effects within organizations: impact (large-scale, sustainable improvements) and visibility (proving that sustainability is in the DNA of the company). The best innovations are visible to stakeholders and have a large impact. Product-based innovations that are visible to clients would qualify in this category. However, these are often the most challenging innovations. As the Innovator, it is up to the CSR or CSO manager to ensure that these innovations are initiated and implemented. Or, when they are initiated by someone else, to support and guide them towards success.

FIGURE 7.3 **Innovations with impact and visibility**

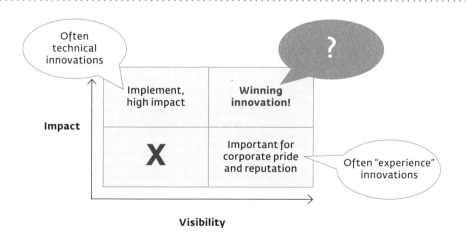

133

Key tasks as the Innovator are to keep the long-term perspective and to be persistent. Innovations are often deprioritized due to more urgent short-term issues and, unfortunately, sustainable innovations tend to take some time to prove their value or to deliver any return on investment.

The CSR or CSO manager, thinking from the outside in, should be aware of innovation trends outside the company and their possibilities and impacts. Frameworks for responsible innovations are developed to address possible social and ethical concerns. At the same time, the introduction of disruptive technologies can boost the possibilities and impacts dramatically.

Kate Brandt (Google Sustainability Officer):

> *"As we move from a conceptual circular economy to implementation, new technologies — particularly AI and machine learning — enable some of these new circular business or products. For our own operations we've been using machine learning. Applying a machine algorithm to our cooling system in our data centers for instance, resulted in a 30% increase in efficiency."*

7.2   Initiating and guiding innovation in practice

Horizons 1 and 2: optimization and renewal

At NS, many first and second horizon innovations came from within the organization; for example, innovations to facilitate more energy-efficient ways to drive the trains or intelligent lighting systems for trains and platforms. But innovation with external partners also falls into this category: working with network operator ProRail on a project to adjust the voltage on the grid will deliver large sustainability and operational efficiency gains.

NS used to have no clear, central approach for capturing and using innovative ideas from employees. Each individual business unit had its own idea management approach to capturing and guiding ideas to implementation. Each business unit also had its own incubator, with resources available to innovate in specific areas, potentially with external partners.

An example of horizon 1 innovation with stakeholders is the aforementioned Low Car Diet, co-created with Urgenda, the NGO famous for winning a historic climate lawsuit. The guidance of such an innovation journey takes a lot of effort and patience, so it is important to focus on innovation processes that will have a large impact. The Low Car Diet took at least three years of development before having a real impact.

Horizon 3: creating new products and services

In the context of risk-averse structures of companies like NS, it is challenging to drive innovation. If processes are geared towards operational excellence and not towards creating new products and business models, it is hard to find a way to come up with the innovations needed to achieve the sustainability goals. Yet innovation is crucial to be able to address the changing needs of society and to continue to add value in social, environmental and economic ways. One way to break through this is to organize innovations outside the company, by engaging knowledge hubs, cooperation with science park incubators, or (co-)founding or joining innovations investment funds.

For example, as a sustainability department, we invested in the development of knowledge around influencing human behavior with respect to mobility by asking a knowledge hub to come up with proposals for renewal that are not based on the current systems and structures. And following the example of the French Railways, an external innovation investment fund was joined as well. This fund focused on generating new mobility products and services that are not yet part of the current portfolio. Sustainability was a criterion in the selection process for the investments, but not an objective in itself. Over the years, the latter changed, fueled by the growing need for sustainable innovations; for instance, in the field of circular materials.

Visible innovations in practice

At NS, examples of a very visible innovation are the serving trays created out of outdated railway schedules (as shown in Figure 7.4) and bags made out of recycled upholstery from the train seats. These products, among other up-cycled products, are frequently sold in pop-up stores at stations. As long as the systems behind such initiatives are valid, such small-scale innovations bring the story of recycling waste and circular economy to life. Telling the story of the reuse of the materials, it works wonderfully to upcycle materials into nice eye-catching well-designed products, which can be displayed at visible points in your organization. Following the success of the serving trays, the floors of trains are now used for football tables (as shown in Figure 7.4), located in stations and canteens, to show that almost 100% of all the material of refurbished trains are reused in new trains or different products without grinding it into granulate or other raw materials.

Other great examples of innovations that are both visible and have an impact are often sustainable (office) buildings, such as the Edge, of accountancy

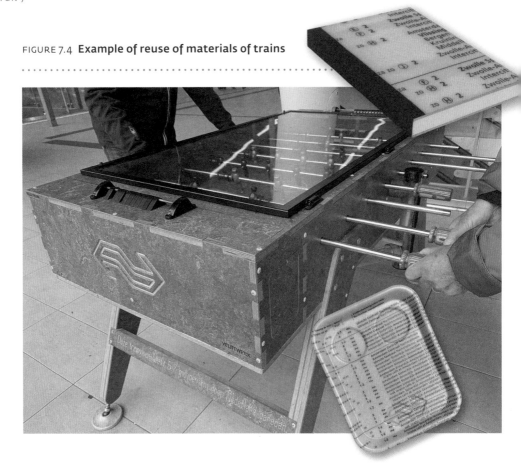

FIGURE 7.4 **Example of reuse of materials of trains**

firm Deloitte and meeting center, the CirCl of ABN AMRO bank: both located in the financial area of Amsterdam. These buildings are designed and constructed according to the sustainable and circular principles and, as such, are easy to disassemble, making as little impact as possible on the planet. A further development is "positive impact" performance standards for buildings — to give more than they take — like "The Living Building Challenge" standard.

Pia Heidenmark Cook (Chief Sustainability Officer Ingka Group):

"Sustainability is about understanding the constraints and opportunities around you and turn them into opportunities. Climate change, inequality and unsustainable consumption patterns are interdependently connected and contribute to our life at home (and in society at large). Understanding these trends and how it impacts

the IKEA business is key in our sustainability work, where innovation and business development are key parts of our sustainability agenda.

We are testing on several markets new clean energy services: from selling solar panels, heat pumps etc. to customers, to testing urban farming solutions for food served in our stores to new circular offers like furniture as a service and second-hand market. Fundamentally, it is about understanding people's needs and dreams in life at home and finding solutions that fits within one planet living to meet these needs."

7.3 The learning Innovator

When it comes to the Innovator role, lessons learned are numerous, since the Innovator role is different in each company and often a learning process in itself. However, I would like to share the following (limited) learning of CSOs as Innovators.

One of my first lessons as an Innovator was that, to achieve innovation in the field of sustainability, I had to make it continuously clear that the apparently comfortable position of our lead was only of short duration: that a difference or gap emerges between what the company delivers and what the customer or stakeholder demands. There are different ways of dealing with this; among other things, it is possible to make visible the development of the competitors' sustainability and to compare it with your own pace of development. The simplicity of Figure 7.4 has been of help. The fact that the sustainable lead rapidly disappears gives a boost to the need for sustainable renewal.

The question, "what would nature do?" might be useful when searching for innovative solutions for a sustainability challenge at product, process and system level. For example, inspired by a particular type of forest foliage, Interface developed the concept of carpet tiles with a random design, so that they can be placed non-directionally, minimizing loss from cutting. Importantly, it makes it easier to partially replace carpet tiles, thus increasing the usage period and reducing the environmental impact. Futhermore, this concept increases the potential reuse of carpet tiles as well. The carpet tiles based on this design principle now represent more than 40% of their sales volume.

Some concepts are successful and others are not, especially when investigating radical improvements. Affording engineers and designers the opportunity to take risks by investing in their ideas might lead to groundbreaking solutions. Such solutions require courage — and people need to feel free to both succeed and fail.

Investigating the boundaries of an individual company increases the chances of discovering new and effective processes. People with knowledge, expertise, and experience — even from completely different sectors — can sometimes provide the missing piece of the puzzle. A good example is Net-Works[18], an inclusive circular business model, which is a partnership between Interface, the Zoological Society of London and Aquafil, a yarn manufacturer. Since 2012, local fishermen in the Danajon Bank in the Philippines have collected discarded fishing nets and Interface processes them into carpet tiles. The fishing community on these islands is among the poorest in the world. The region is of great ecological value because of the special coral reef and the coast, but that diversity is threatened by overfishing and pollution. The project therefore kills several birds with one stone. It removes ghost fishing nets from the sea and the beaches, restores biodiversity and improves the living conditions of fishermen. The yarn factory, in turn, found a suitable waste stream for its plan to recycle more nylon and the carpet manufacturer is making carpet tiles from yarn with 100% recycled nylon. In this way, it had come a step closer to its ambition to make a restorative contribution to the environment and society by 2020. Moreover, lessons learned are shared in the Nextwaveplastics[19] initiative, set up by Dell and joined by many manufacturers, such as HP and IKEA to prevent other types of plastics getting into the oceans.

FIGURE 7.5 **Philips's Circular Innovation — LAAS** (Ellen MacArthur Foundation case study)

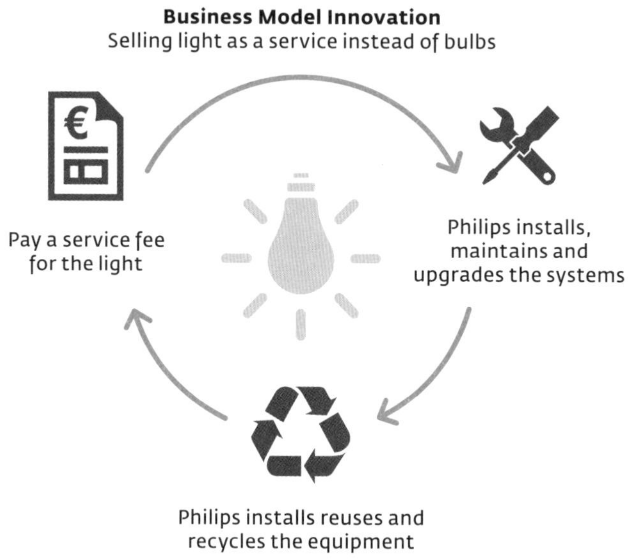

Business Model Innovation
Selling light as a service instead of bulbs

Pay a service fee
for the light

Philips installs,
maintains and
upgrades the systems

Philips installs reuses and
recycles the equipment

And last but not least, it is key to make sustainability very relevant for the innovation department and connect it with the company's core business. As early as 1994, Philips had applied EcoDesign, an approach that considers all aspects of product development and design. Nowadays Philips also applies circular economy principles in designing the solutions and new business models, such as Light as a Service (LAAS), as is shown in Figure 7.5.

In 2012, Philips set an ambitious target: by 2030 to have improved the lives of three billion people annually by making the world healthier and more sustainable through innovation. And according to their own report, they still are on track.

7.4 The successful Innovator

The Innovator role is an evolving one for a CSO. Often, CSOs that support their firm's transition to the more mature phase of sustainability by shaping the firm's sustainability strategy (Strategic role) and mastering the art of overseeing "the never-ending evolution" of the business case, also are in the position to help develop the innovation strategy of the firm. The Innovator role is, for many CSOs, the most inspiring role because, as Diane Holdorf (former CSO of Kellogg Company) says:

> *"Innovation drives business,
> and when it clicks, it is exciting."*

There are many great examples of companies where sustainability is a key driver for innovations. One of those companies is Levi Strauss & Co. At Levi's, sustainability is a driver for innovations in various ways:

1   Production innovations. To give an example: the innovation center in the headquarters invented a laser technique to create the denim finishes. This technique saves time and has less impact on the environment and people, lead times and inventories are reduced because the product can be made closer to the market, and customer satisfaction is increased because quality is higher.
2   Design innovations. To give an example: the innovation center is working on the R&D to use more recycled cotton in new products.
3   Longer-term design and business model challenges. To give an example: searching for business innovations to reach the sustainability goals such as full circularity. These business innovations might come from startups, incubated by the company.

The most important assignment of the CSO is to embed operational responsibility for sustainability into the routine operations of the company. This includes innovations centers, research & development, the design team and other innovative powers in a company. For an increasing number of designers, sustainability is an inspirational driver for innovation, something that can be noticed by the growing amount of sustainable innovations at the yearly Dutch Design Week.

As Michael Kobori (former VP Sustainability at Levi Strauss & Co.) puts it:

"It is my experience that design people are creative and very passionate about sustainability. They want to make beautiful things that add to the quality of life, including social and environmental aspects of it. The role of the CSO is to team up, to facilitate their innovation power with necessary knowledge and sometimes tools. To give an example: we developed a tool supporting them in eliminating chemicals from the production process."

A sustainable innovation strategy might affect the entire business and value chain. In an interview in *Dezeen*[20] Inter IKEA group Chief Sustainability Officer Lena Pripp-Kovac explains that they are looking at a total change of their business. Prolonging the life of products and materials is something that designers at IKEA are now putting to the forefront of the design process. The "idea of circular" is already in the design phase, when you think that you have to incorporate the whole life cycle into what you do and how it is owned and what is going to happen with it. She continued that it is also important you put it in the context of an economy. As a big company you cannot be a circular economy all by yourself. You need to have a network and fit into the society in order to have a circular economy.

Purpose-driven innovation

Sustainability champion DSM could be used as a best practice for all 7 Roles, but it is an outstanding practice, if it comes to the Innovator role. It has created sustainable success over the years by reinventing and transforming its business to the most developed maturity phase of sustainability. DSM has fully embedded its purpose, to "create brighter lives for all," in its innovation and science workforce and processes with the company actively displaying leadership on large social issues. Sustainability is driving its science and innovation ecosystem and its business model. With that, DSM has created remarkable solutions to address several of the world's biggest challenges —

as it states, "purpose-led" and "performance-driven" — focusing on creating a positive societal impact in the domains of Nutrition & Health (SDG 2 and 3), Climate & Energy (SDG 7 and 13) and Resources & Circularity (SDG 12). In an open innovation approach, DSM uses all the scientific and innovation power it has along with that of its partners. A great example of translating its purpose into actions is reflected in DSM's innovations to provide nutrition for the most vulnerable people in the world, such as micronutrient powders and fortified rice. These powders are designed for infants and children over six months of age, who have a clear vitamin deficiency which often leads to health issues that cause physical and mental "stunting". They can be mixed directly into any ready-to-eat semi-solid food to boost the micronutrient content of the diet. The goal for 2050 is that DSM's innovative sustainable alternative solutions are no longer "alternatives", but mainstream products across the world. To ensure the full product portfolio is creating a positive impact, the company constantly monitors the environmental and social impacts of its product portfolio. In 2019, more than 60% of sales were called "Brighter Living Solutions", representing products that have a measurably better social or environmental impact than competing solutions.

Is the future of technology the future of sustainability?

Whether or not technology will enable us to reach the Sustainable Development Goals and to adapt to climate change, there are already great examples of how technology can be a solution. In Microsoft's program Artificial Intelligence (AI) for Earth, grants are awarded to support projects that use AI to change the way people and organizations monitor, model, and manage Earth's natural systems.

Wineke Haagsma, Director Corporate Sustainability PwC The Netherlands & EMEA, shares her view on the relation between innovation and sustainability:

"Sustainability requires an innovative mind. You are continuously seeking new ways to contribute to people, the planet and the bottom line. This requires an innovative mind to bring those worlds together and find the sweet spot where we all benefit. With the development of our VR immersive experience, the SDG Dome, we want to bring the Sustainable Development Goals closer to our business, to our people, to our clients. After visiting Singularity University, I was deeply touched by the way VR engages people. Also, we strongly believe that solutions from emerging technologies and your own personal behavior can have a huge impact in the achievement of the SDGs."

Renewable energy — wind for the trains -Innovator role

Environmental stakeholders like Greenpeace, Friends of the Earth Netherlands and Natuur & Milieu called the "wind for the trains" partnership a gamechanger. Following the stakeholder dialogues with NGOs, the aim was also to boost the energy transition and initiate movement in the market. In my Innovator role, I had to find a new way of sourcing to make that happen. Analyzing the energy market and various market consultations showed that we could improve the business case of new renewable parks for developers in two ways:

- By agreeing to a long-term purchasing agreement, the business case for the renewable power plants becomes stronger, decreasing the risk and the cost of capital
- The characteristics of trains' use of energy, the tremendous size of the contract — 1.4 TWh per year for ten years, which is about the same size as the use of the households of Amsterdam — and the solid credit rating of NS: with this the credit rating of the supplier also improved, facilitating the financing of new renewable energy plants.

A boost for a more sustainable energy sector could therefore be achieved by entering into a ten-year renewables contract instead of the normal practice of:

- short-term procurement horizon, and
- sourcing energy and renewables (certificates) separately from different plants.

In order to attract the "right" partner, a strategic fit was required at the beginning of the tendering process.

From the strategic framework developed in the Coordinator role, renewables from additional and traceable plants were specified, so that we knew exactly from where the renewables would come. This resulted in an offer of plants that were already planned, but not yet in production, with a direct connection to the grid. These plants, once they came into operation, fed 1.4 TWh of wind power into the same grid that the trains take their electricity from, balancing volumes on a yearly basis.

Ultimately, this tender led to the largest wind power contract in Europe, ready to deliver one year earlier than planned. It also continues to generate new activities, as the partnership calls for a joint and continuous search for more sustainable opportunities, together with the supplier, Eneco.

By innovating activities, you can initiate changes that lead to sustainable adjustments in the systems. The renewable power contract for Dutch trains provides a great example. Nowadays many other companies and organizations use the same innovative sourcing strategy. Together with new energy-producing partner Eneco, which invested in the new parks, we contributed to a shift in the system by using an innovative sourcing strategy.

CEO tied to a windmill
Not only was the contract itself innovative, but also the way it was communicated. The Netherlands is believed to be the first country in the world to have its trains running on 100% wind power. However, it only became world news when it was communicated by Roger van Boxtel, CEO of NS in a very unusual way: he presented the news in a video while he was tied to a windmill that was running on wind power. People often ask me, "how did you persuade your CEO to do this?" The answer is that I did not had to, because he was already so enthusiastic that he wanted to find a unique way to spread the word. Thanks to the communications department, the video was not only made but, over the years, there were already so many facts communicated through more traditional channels, that journalists could use these facts to fill their own news items in papers and televisions, using the publicity created by the video.

This high-impact and system-changing innovation had a very stimulating effect on other sustainable innovations and communications because it fueled the pride of employees, like it fueled the pride of the CEO, who did not need to be convinced to climb into a windmill at all!

Tips for Innovators

- Map the innovation process in your company, so you can embed sustainability within it.
- Ensure you have plenty of ideas and innovations in the pipeline, as only a few will be implemented.
- Adjust the way you approach the Innovator role to the maturity of the organization regarding innovation and sustainability.
- Mobilize internal innovation power by positioning sustainability as an urgent driver for innovation. Highlight the difference between the sustainable future of the company and where it is today.
- Arrange a sufficient number of internal stakeholders that share this sense of urgency.
- Leverage internal innovation processes by including sustainability as a selection criterion.
- Plot on different timelines and horizons; real breakthrough innovations take time.
- If there is no room for third horizon innovations within the company, arrange an external innovations process.
- Innovations get better by collaborating with others. Use an open innovation approach to access external available scientific and innovation power.
- Ask the question, what would nature do? when searching for innovative solutions for a sustainability challenge at product, process and system level.
- Groundbreaking solutions require courage and people need to feel free to both succeed and fail.
- Ensure you also include visual innovations.
- Be persistent. Innovation does not just apply to the golden idea, creativity is also necessary to ensure key projects continue, which might otherwise not make it in the turmoil of short-term priorities.
- Shield people with innovative ideas from overly critical people and from endless administrative procedures by connecting them to relevant sponsors within the company.
- Make sure the Initiator of an idea remains the owner. For great ideas, support the process, but do not take over.
- Invest energy to turn that winning idea into success, rather than investing it only in the prevention of unsuccessful innovations.
- Make use of existing innovation processes as much as possible to avoid the "not invented here" syndrome.
- Be aware of innovation trends outside the company and their possibilities and impacts. The introduction of disruptive technologies can change impacts dramatically.

The Monitor

"However beautiful the strategy, you should occasionally look at the results."

WINSTON CHURCHILL (1874-1965), FORMER PRIME MINISTER OF THE UNITED KINGDOM

For accountability purposes and to keep steering and guiding the sustainability achievements of the organization, you need information. The CSO needs to ensure this information is reliable, useful, relevant and measurable.

"I consider CSOs learners rather than Monitors. We learn from data. When it comes to reducing our environmental footprint, we know what areas to focus on because we've studied our impact and have data to drive our decisions."

MICHAEL KOBORI (FORMER VP SUSTAINABILITY AT LEVI STRAUSS & CO.)

The Monitor role includes monitoring and evaluating (applications of) the sustainability strategy and policies, such as setting up internal audits and establishing internal measurement methodologies. In the Monitor role, the CSO often contributes to the sustainability content of the annual report or a separate sustainability report. There are several relevant regulations, governance tools and guidelines available to fulfill this part of the Monitor role.

To be a good Monitor, a CSO, CSR or sustainability manager needs the competency of "instrumental thinking", requiring strong analytical skills and the ability to understand/or develop instruments, standards and procedures for sustainable activities, specifically those used to monitor and measure impact or disclose information. The implementation of the Monitor role will differ from company to company. For example, in listed companies, specific people might be assigned to the area of sustainability reporting. This role is then often assigned to someone with either a financial or communications background.

The most important task as a Monitor is to collect information (measurement) which helps to guide (reporting and improvement) the sustainability strategy and with which the company can be accountable to its stakeholders. In order to do this, the CSO needs to proactively collect, analyze and act upon relevant data. Data related to sustainability performance can be divided into in several categories, such as environmental and social impact and corporate governance. This chapter highlights the role and organization of sustainability information, the importance of data and metrics, as well as the most relevant tasks for the CSO in the Monitor role.

8.1 The role of sustainability information

The availability of information is crucial for the integration of sustainability into the organization. It helps to:

- Make achievements visible
- Support a positive business case
- Share with stakeholders how much progress has been made on their material topics
- Make better-informed decisions, such as adjusting plans if it becomes clear that goals will not be achieved.

Sustainability information needs to be useful (transparent, accessible, relevant), measurable and reliable (accurate). "Numbers never lie" but the numbers have to be reliable, as there are people who like to play with them. As Winston Churchill said:

> *"I only believe in statistics I doctored myself."*

Sustainability metrics and indicators

To deliver such information, quantifiable measurements of activities are needed. A key question for the CSO or CSR manager is: "What to measure?" "Which metric to track?" The answer to these questions starts with the key performance indicators, such as those shared in Table 4.1. It is an important task for the CSO or CSR manager (as a Coordinator) to match these indicators with the focus areas and the progress you want to achieve in each of these areas, as defined in the Network and Strategist role. Similar companies or peers in the industry using sustainability metrics and indicators are a good source of inspiration when selecting metrics. In 2014, in a review[21] of sustainability metrics, entitled "The growth of sustainability metrics," the Earth Institute (Columbia University) had already identified close to two hundred indicators in each of three categories — environmental, social and governance — resulting in 557 total indicators or metrics. Other sources of inspiration are more general indicator frameworks related to specific goals; for example, the SDGs or reviews of trends in corporate sustainability reporting, such as are incorporated in the annual State of Green Business Report by Greenbiz.[22] For some metrics or indicators, you can also make use of assessments or measurements by third parties, such as ratings, supplier assessments, reputation trackers or benchmarks like the Dow Jones Sustainability Index.

As a Monitor you have to ensure that ownership (responsibility and accountability) of the indicators and the underlying metrics are secured at the right level in the organization and that the underlying values are measurable. In companies, the term metric is often used synonymously with indicator. In this chapter, I use metrics as a more general (calculation) method to understand change over time, supporting the KPI or performance indicators that keep track of progress on the key sustainability goal(s). The source of metrics and indicators are measures of values such as use of electricity or waste in bins.

Eventually, the data generated should provide useful information when tracking progress and making necessary adjustments to plans or strategies. For some KPIs, there will be a specific, realistic (usually time-bound) goal or target set, but this is not always the case. Both the KPI and the goal or target should be measurable and acceptable. When selecting indicators, it is key to align them with existing business governance processes, such as the planning and control cycle and the appraisal processes.

For data collection and the calculations required for an indicator, you need to determine and agree on the processes as well as establish owners who are responsible for this. Again, it is smart to align with existing processes. An example of this is aligning metrics with units that are invoiced by suppliers. With suppliers, you can agree on the required information so that the relevant values automatically enter the financial system and serve as a source for sustainability information. Definitions of measures, sources, methods, should be made explicit and documented in a handbook that is regularly updated. Value measured can come from more than one system and explicit definitions of the sustainability information are important to guarantee the reliability of the information. Additionally, it will strengthen the status of sustainability indicators as serious key performance business indicators.

Global trends on transparency ask for more reliable sustainability information about the entire supply chain. To use the example of the food and beverage industry: sustainability information related to transparency about food ingredients has become a crucial driver for business, since customers increasingly want to know what they are eating. In addition, NGOs proactively started assessing and ranking companies on a wide range of sustainability issues, such as Oxfam's "Behind the Brands campaign."[23] In this campaign, the ten biggest food and beverage companies were rated on how their supply chain policies address seven key issue areas: land rights, women's rights, support for small farmers, workers' rights, climate, transparency, and water, encompassing over three hundred indicators. More recently, a similar campaign called "Behind the Barcodes" has been launched focusing on supermarkets and human rights.

The control cycle

The Plan-Do-Check-Act model (Figure 8.1) is a method used in business for the control and continuous improvement of processes and products. From the strategy, requirements or frameworks are established, upon which plans are created for business units and departments (Plan). Plans are then executed (Do) and lead to results (Outputs). The progress of these results is measured and based on the correct measures of progress and quality (Check) the people responsible will modify their efforts (Act).

This model can be applied to track and steer the progress on the implementation of the sustainability strategy. It can also be used to asses and further the maturity of (integrating) sustainability in organizations.

- *Plan*: as the Coordinator, the CSR or CSO manager focuses on creating the sustainability plan with focus areas and KPIs
- *Do*: as the Stimulator and Mentor, the CSR or CSO manager focuses on the implementation of the sustainability plan
- *Check*: as the Monitor, (s)he focuses on the measurement of sustainability achievements
- *Act*: based on the collected information, the responsible managers can adjust or modify the plans as necessary. If sustainability is fully embedded in an organization the role of the CSO, CSR or sustainability manager is limited.

FIGURE 8.1 **Plan-Do-Check-Act circle**

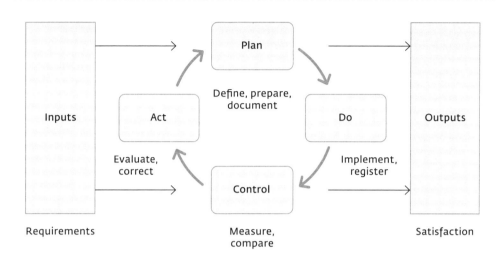

The role of the CSO, CSR or sustainability manager is to close this control cycle, so the strategic targets can be achieved. When sustainability is well embedded into the organization, the responsibility to act and modify efforts lies not with the sustainability team, but with other managers in the organization. The CSO, CSR or sustainability manager is, of course, directly responsible for any modifications regarding the integration of sustainability in the organization. In some (large) companies, an internal audit to assess (integration of) the sustainability strategy and policies can be a useful (but intensive!) instrument to determine which modifications are needed.

In case you can make use of existing reporting, measurement and control systems, such as balanced score card, OGSM planning cycles or any other management control system, it is the task of the CSR or CSO manager to monitor the sustainability-related elements in these systems and to ensure that the relevant responsible (business) managers modify their plans when targets are not achieved. Modifications can include speeding up certain measures or adding more sustainable elements to planned activities.

It is key to measure and monitor high impact metrics more frequently than those with a lower impact in order to give managers the opportunity to modify or adjust plans when needed to achieve targets. That means, for instance, that the energy use of the trains is monitored monthly, as it accounts for 85% of the total usage. The remaining energy use is monitored on an annual basis.

On a less frequent basis (for example, every other year), the strategy and the goals can be adjusted. This also incorporates stakeholder feedback, causing an overlap with the Networker role. When stakeholders adjust their expectations or see new opportunities, there may be reason to also adjust the material topics and hence the strategic plan.

Social impact measurement methods

Many different social impact measurement methods exist (Maas & Liket[24], 2011). These methods have been developed in response to the changing needs for management information resulting from the increased interest of corporations in socially responsible activities. The social impact measurement methods were found to differ on the following dimensions: *purpose, time frame, orientation, length of time frame, perspective* and *approach*. Depending on these characteristics, different indicators will be used and therefore different impacts will be measured. One of the impact measurement methods often used in practice is LCA (Ewen, Maas & Toxopeus[25], 2019). Life Cycle Analysis or Assessment (LCA) analyses the impacts associated with products, or product systems. LCA has its origins in the early seventies. The method had its roots in energy and waste management and the products given greatest attention in this initial period were beverage containers and diapers. In the period 1980-2000, the main focus of LCA was solely on environmental aspects. During the last decades, partnerships of academia and practitioners have developed an approach to incorporate social aspects in LCAs.[26]

Life cycle analysis (LCA)

The LCA is a method that maps the influence of products and human activity on the environment. LCA considers all stages in the product's life cycle, from the sourcing of raw materials through to product manufacture, distribution, product's use and disposal. LCA is often used as the baseline from which to set targets. It provides a clear picture of the product's main environmental impacts. These are often outside of the company. For example, the energy use of an appliance or car usually causes more CO_2 emissions than the manufacturing process.

There are many standardized LCA approaches for specific sectors, enabling companies to communicate their environmental impact more objectively; for example, through product-level environmental declarations. The sustainability strategic framework can be built upon an LCA, focusing on the part(s) of a company or product's life cycle framework that has the biggest impact. The outcomes of the analysis, therefore, support the CSO in the Coordinator role (Chapter 4), such as in the case of Levi's, which is shown in paragraph 8.4 of this chapter.

The biggest impact of your product, however, might not be in the gift of your company's direct influence. To give an example, Unilever's model (introduced in Chapter 5) "5 levers of change" has been designed for changing consumer behavior. LCA made them understand that consumer-use impact is big and that managing this impact is crucial to achieve their Sustainable Living Plan goals.

With the outcomes of LCA, usually the discussion about scoping of goals, baseline and strategic framework is started.

Sustainability reporting

During the past decades, there has been a tremendous development in the field of sustainability reporting, especially investors fueling demand for standardized sustainability data and more of it. In the reporting and investor worlds, "sustainability" is measured in three distinct categories: environmental, social, and governance: otherwise known as ESG.

- Environmental disclosures focus on topics like greenhouse gas emissions, such as CO_2 emissions and fine particulates next to water usage, waste disposal and more
- Social disclosures include information about diversity and inclusion, labor relations, product safety, employee health and safety and other relevant information such as community development
- Governance disclosures focuses on good practice information such as ethics, board diversity and composition, shareholder rights, supply chain engagement.

Measures to respond to growing investor demands for more uniform sustainability information linked to financial performance of global companies are taken by regulatory bodies and stock exchanges around the world. The European Commission has made sustainability reporting mandatory for all large companies through the EU Directive on Non-Financial Reporting.[27] Companies that operate in EU member states and meet certain criteria are required to disclose information on the way they operate and manage social and environmental challenges.

In addition, a number of initiatives are underway to advance greater standardization and transparency of sustainability disclosures. Two such frameworks are the Global Reporting Initiative (GRI) and Integrated Reporting (IR).

The GRI process focuses on the selection of sustainability topics that make a difference or "matter" for the company creating a sustainability report. The emphasis is on providing information that is essential for the company and for the stakeholders, the so-called material topics. The GRI Standards provide indicators for most environmental, social, governance and economic topics. In addition to the company-specific selection of topics and the corresponding indicators, a GRI report should also include a general set of topics.[28]

Integrated reporting has a different focus: making clear how an organization creates economic, social and environmental value, now and in the future. To achieve this, an organization need to be transparent on how it takes the various capitals into account in creating this value, as well as the external environment, mutual relationships and dependencies.[29]

Also, two other initiatives respond to growing investor demands for more uniform sustainability information: the Sustainability Accounting Standards Board (SASB) and the Task Force on Climate-Related Financial Disclosures.

The SASB is a US-based and independent organization whose mission is to develop and disseminate sustainability accounting standards that help public corporations disclose material information useful to the investor. And the Task Force on Climate-Related Financial Disclosures is an industry-led body that has developed recommendations for voluntary climate-related disclosures that are consistent, comparable, and provide useful information to investors, lenders, insurers and other stakeholders.

The Greenhouse Gas Protocol (GHGP)[30] is considered to be the most important and common standard for registering greenhouse gas emissions at company level. It provides accounting and reporting standards on how companies and organizations should capture and report in a standardized way for greenhouse gas emissions. Two types of "boundaries" are important for reporting: organizational and operational boundaries. The organizational boundary must first be determined. What does the organization have control or ownership of? Then the operational boundary (scope 1, scope 2, scope 3), of this organization boundary is determined, and the associated direct and indirect emissions. In short:

- *Scope 1*: Direct GHG emissions from sources that are owned or controlled by the company; for example, emissions from combustion in owned or controlled boilers, furnaces, vehicles, etc.; emissions from chemical production in owned or controlled process equipment.
- *Scope 2*: Electricity indirect GHG emissions. Scope 2 accounts for GHG emissions from the generation of purchased electricity consumed by the company. Purchased electricity is defined as electricity that is purchased or otherwise brought into the organizational boundary of the company. Scope 2 emissions physically occur at the facility where electricity is generated.

- *Scope 3*: Other indirect GHG emissions. Scope 3 emissions are a consequence of the activities of the company, but occur from sources not owned or controlled by the company. Some examples of scope 3 activities are: extraction and production of purchased materials, transportation of purchased fuels and use of sold products and services.

The GHGP has been used by many companies as well as the by the International Organization for Standardization (ISO) as basis for ISO certification. The GHGP was initiated by the World Resources Institute (WRI), a think tank for environmental protection, and by the World Business Council for Sustainable Development (WBCSD), an association of companies in the field of sustainable development.

To sum up, there is a wealth of information and guidance available on how to report non-financial information in the annual reporting cycle, but there is no single sustainability standard in the market today. There remains a certain level of market confusion as to the purpose and use of these standards, including questions on how to determine materiality and how disclosures should be presented (e.g., standalone report, survey response, annual report or financial filing). A clear trend in all reporting developments, however, is to focus on what matters and where it matters and to show how this information is used to run the company and to create value for stakeholders.

Next to the voluntary and — in case of the EU directive — mandatory disclosures and above platforms, there are a growing number of environmental, social and governance (ESG) ratings firms that assess and score ESG disclosures, such as Sustainalytics, Institutional Shareholder Services and MSCI. In most cases, companies are automatically rated and these ratings are then sold to interested third parties or mass media. They list these so-called sustainability scores, which are often used for quick ESG assessments of companies by investors and other stakeholders.

Although recent research shows that sustainability reporting for large public companies around the world has become the norm[31], there are still many companies that do not report. In their Monitor role, CSOs should understand and prepare their boards of directors for the implications of growing ESG transparency and the opportunities and risks that follow on from the increased interest in sustainability information, of investors and other stakeholders. For some CSOs, this might be the first time that they actually get board-level attention. The World Economic Forum's Global Risks Report, released in January 2018, notes that environmental concerns top the global risk list again.

Todd Cort, Lecturer Sustainability at Yale School of Management:

> *"Investors have taken an increased role in pushing for disclosure and action on sustainability information from companies. This represents a great opportunity for CSOs to bring sustainability to the boardroom. Understanding and preparing their boards of directors for the implications of growing ESG transparency and the opportunities and risks that follow from it, can be a first step in raising boardroom awareness about the strategic relevance of sustainability."*

Monetization of societal impact

The consequences of business activities on society such as health, education, environment and community are called its environmental and social impact. Impact or outcome is different from output such as products or services in that it "adds" its effect to society. Figure 2.2 shows the elemental impact of NS, such as the health benefits of train and bike rides, due to cleaner air and more exercise for its users. For a purpose-driven company, it can be more relevant to define a purpose-related KPI and to measure impact instead of output.

Impact of business activities can be measured and valued in various ways. A relatively new way to display the sustainability achievements of a company is to calculate and express the societal impact (environmental and social impact) in financial values: the costs and benefits generated by a company that would not show up in a regular annual report. These costs or benefits or external effects of a company on third parties, for which they did not choose or ask, are often referred to as externalities. For example, environmental externalities arise because, in most cases, no one has property rights to the environment and nature and, therefore, no one really feels responsible for taking good care of it, the so-called *tragedy of the commons*.

Effects can be both positive and negative. An example of a positive externality is when a company invests in infrastructure and parks around the office, from which the community also benefits free of charge. An example of a negative externality is a company emitting CO_2, for which the societal costs are higher (for example through global warming) than the calculated costs for that company. By translating all such externalities to euros or another currency, you can monetize these effects. Monetization provides insight into social and environmental profit and loss, in addition to the financial profit and loss statements.

To determine which effects are most relevant to the societal impact of your company, the material topics can be used again. You can focus calculations on the effects which matter most according to your stakeholders and are relevant to your business. If you want to calculate the impact of a company, the environmental profit and loss statement is a logical starting point. For example, Vodafone Netherlands (now VodafoneZiggo) and Puma calculated their environmental impacts and published an environmental profit and loss statement. To monetize the impact on the product level so that the "price" is comparable for a buyer or consumer, more standardization is needed, such as product category rules to conduct comparable LCAs.

The Monitor role is a very relevant role for the CSO, feeding relevant data into all other roles. Moreover, it will increase even further in relevance when the transition of the company towards sustainable business develops. Introducing circular business models and new sustainable investment models then requires additional financial skills to understand the consequences of these new business models for the key financial metrics and accounting standards of your company.

8.2 Measuring, reporting and adjusting in practice

During the last few years, I have spent a significant amount of my time as CSO in the Monitor role. It is not the one that comes most naturally to me, but it has proven to be very effective for the integration of sustainability and in generating support, all because it enabled me to share visible results and progress quite quickly.

Handbook sustainability information

To embed the process of producing reliable sustainability metrics, it should be clear — step by step — how and by whom the sustainability metric is produced, which data is used, which source, what calculation method and who is responsible for what. The more complex the metric, the more extensive the process and the need to be very precise and transparent about it; this eventually results in a handbook. As stated earlier, it is effective to find sources and owners of data that are aligned with, and responsible for, other financial business processes, such as invoices of suppliers. For instance, for the NS annual report, the following defined measured values are used for traction energy use per passenger kilometer:

- Annual number of passenger kilometers: a passenger travelling one kilometer by train is defined as one passenger kilometer. All passengers, on all their journeys, on all trains of NS within the Netherlands per year, altogether generate the annual number of passenger kilometers of NS.

- The passenger kilometers are also used as a basis for balancing income between carriers, for example for the public transport annual pass (OV chip). The passenger kilometers are determined by carrying out spot checks in trains (passenger surveys) and analyzing check in/check out transactions of the OV chip card and via Nobot.
- Traction energy use: kilowatt hours (kWh) are used. The financial control units are the source for this data, based on the invoices of the energy provider and a calculation model by a trusted third party to split the usage — adjusted for weather conditions by including "degree days" — into trains of the different operators on the Dutch rail network. The kWhs metrics are measured at the terminals of the substations of the grid (not at the trains), thus including energy losses due to transportation from substations to pantograph of the trains and transformation to the 1500 Volt grid.

Growing ESG transparency

In 2010, sustainability was integrated into NS's strategy, and started with the mantra of "measurement for knowledge". It turned out that there was quite some activity already and that many things were measured, but there was a clear lack of focus and cohesion. Environmental indicators were not included in the regular reporting cycle, nor in the business planning cycle. My focus, therefore, was on the integration of this environmental data in the business planning, and the planning and control cycle. I also wanted to create an overview of all sustainability-related activities to support the Coordinator role. The development of regulation in the field of sustainability reporting for state-owned companies in the Netherlands supported the integration and transparency enormously. Being a state-owned company with an enormous impact on society, NS has a history of reporting on non-financial and financial results in one "integrated" report. However, the real integration of reporting came with the specific standards of GRI. At a gradual pace, year after year, transparency and quality of the sustainability information improved, eventually resulting in a national award for transparency.

Visualization of sustainability information.

You often hear it said, "a picture says a thousand words", and that is also very true if it shows sustainability information. A nice example is the visualization of the carbon footprint of the office of pension fund, PPGM (figure 8.2), showing directly that car rides contribute most to the footprint.

FIGURE 8.2 **Carbon footprint of the office of pension fund PPGM**

Total emission 6.071 ton CO_2

40%
Car travel

29%
Air travel

19% Paper waste

7% Heating

4% Public transport

1% Electricity

FIGURE 8.3 **Societal cost and environmental impact analysis NS**

Negative environmental impact

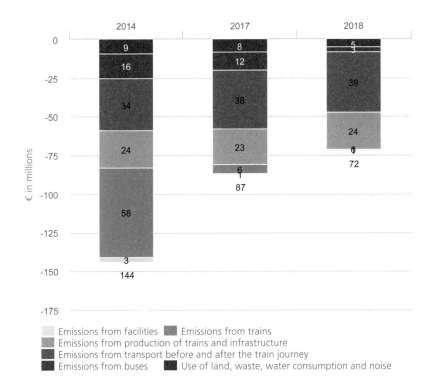

Emissions from facilities   Emissions from trains
Emissions from production of trains and infrastructure
Emissions from transport before and after the train journey
Emissions from buses   Use of land, waste, water consumption and noise

Positive impact with respect to cars

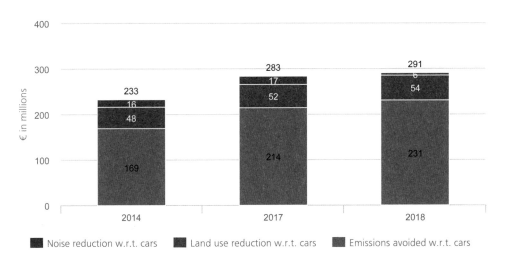

Noise reduction w.r.t. cars   Land use reduction w.r.t. cars   Emissions avoided w.r.t. cars

The NS annual report not only covers the direct and intended effects, but also the unintended and indirect effects related to the materials topics. Since 2014, NS has been calculating and publishing these environmental and socio-economic effects. An example of the visualization of the environmental impact is shown in Figure 8.3. Although less attractive than the footprint of PGGM, it shows directly that negative environmental impact has halved (mainly due to the wind-powered trains), in four years.

8.3 The learning Monitor

The most important lesson to be learned is to integrate sustainable information with the other financial and business information processes, and make the financial department responsible for part of the Monitor role. The sooner the better, since it gives you better information and secures the involvement of the CFO, a crucial internal stakeholder. In the end, reporting will be really relevant when it leads to better informed and more sustainable action. If you can find a way to make sustainability information relevant to the CFO, such as growing ESG transparency, this will start a relationship that can become the backbone of the sustainability integration and investments.

At NS, the relationship between sustainability and finance has led to several successes such as winning a prize, developing a study case for Yale students, publishing a white paper and developing innovations in the field of monetizing impact (triple P & L).

Selecting indicator

One of the biggest challenges in the Monitor role is to determine the right indicators and metrics. Choosing targets and indicators that turn out to be unmanageable, is a pitfall and a good example of this is the reputation goal and the associated indicator. Improving the reputation of NS is an important part of the sustainability business case (Table 3.1). The reputation of NS is measured on the basis of an instrument called RepTrak. Many companies use this measuring instrument to assess their overall reputation. It was assumed that improving the reputation in sustainability would lead to a better overall reputation. To improve the reputation in sustainability by 2020, a CSR goal was also formulated: to be among the top ten most sustainable companies in the Netherlands in the annual survey of a sustainable brands ranking list. This goal got stuck on two points:

▪ There appeared to be no causal positive relationship between the general reputation and sustainable reputation. As our reputation in sustainability improved, our overall reputation did not improve, since it is heavily determined by operational factors. RepTrak does have CSR-related drivers, but they weigh less heavily than other operational factors. Our indicator for reputation in sustainability became, therefore, a separate measuring instrument.

■ This effect was enhanced because our reputation in sustainability is also considerably determined by operational factors and less by CSR performance. Improving the position in the ranking of sustainable brands on the basis of CSR achievements was difficult to grasp and therefore difficult to manage.

The result is that, despite the good results in the field of sustainability, we have not been able to capitalize on this in terms of reputation and, therefore, also less in the commercial area.

Another lesson learned concerned targeted sustainability performance indicators for senior management appraisal reviews. As described earlier, senior management has formulated a targeted sustainability performance indicator for its appraisal reviews. For further implementation there were two options:

■ Determine a performance indicator per job area, which the manager can actually steer and manage

■ Determine a performance indicator per business unit to ensure that everyone within the same business unit had the same targeted sustainability performance indicator and everyone would contribute to achieving the same target.

Although the latter has the advantage that it is obviously a joint effort, the disadvantage of the differences in control was demotivating.

Facts versus beliefs

Sometimes beliefs are so strong that facts and data will not turn the tide. In addition, scientific results can be interpreted in different ways so that there may be more "conflicting" conclusions. When it comes to the use of plastics, the common belief these days is that plastic is bad. Although plastic has positive aspects like its weight, it is not seen as sustainable. The same holds for the use of biomass in coal-fired plants. From the beginning, it was intuitively felt to be an "inferior" way of generating renewable energy. When you feel that these beliefs are strongly held, it is advisable to act and find other solutions.

Beliefs and opinions can get in way of facts and good policy. A subject that certainly triggers opinions and beliefs is waste separation and recycling. Emotional aspects therefore should be included when making policy. Sometimes perceptions can be used as an accelerator for sustainable policy. When

I started as CSO, the facts showed that the train was the most sustainable long-distance mode of transport. However, the perception of our customer was less positive. I used that perception to urge the board to accelerate our sustainability program. As mentioned in Chapter 5 about the Stimulator role, a three-minute video of customers at stations was made, in which they expressed their perception of the train and NS. This video had more impact than any other data, figures or logic I could have brought forward.

Transparency is not the same as integrity

Be aware that, even if your company is very open and transparent in reporting, this does not mean that there will be no fraud or deception. Recently there have been a number of scandals involving reliability of environmental information; for example, on car emissions, such as with Volkswagen. Can a sustainable and transparent company and fraud go together? Even though there is a difference between "doing no harm" (compliance with regulations) and "doing good", it is expected that these go hand in hand. However, the CSO must focus on "doing good" and leaving compliance to the risk manager and internal watchdog. When fraud does happen, transparency is also about the way you communicate openly about your errors and dilemmas and make information available to the public.

8.4 The successful Monitor

Focus on impact – Life Cycle Assessments

Frequently I meet CSOs who would rather forget about their Monitor role. But not Michael Kobori former VP Sustainability at Levi Strauss & Co.:

"In 2006, we presented the outcome of environmental life cycle assessment on a pair of Levi's® 501s to our company leadership and shared our insights and facts. One of our biggest areas of impact – and one of the most critical resources on the planet – is water. From this point of view our assessment was that during the life cycle, the most water is used during the cotton-growing and consumer-care phases. It is hard to argue with data, so based on these insights the company shifted focus. Often executives have their own idea or point of view about what sustainability should be; with these facts, it became clear what our focus should be. We should engage in cotton programs (the Better Cotton Initiative) and encourage consumers to wash less, wash cold, line dry and donate their products when done so that we can use them again."

FIGURE 8.4 **Cradle-to-grave water consumption of a pair of jeans** (A Product Life Cycle Approach to Sustainability, Levi Strauss & Co. San Francisco, CA March 2009)

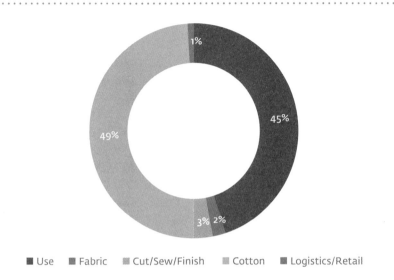

■ Use   ■ Fabric   ■ Cut/Sew/Finish   ■ Cotton   ■ Logistics/Retail

Geanne van Arkel, Head of Sustainable Development of Interface Europe underlines the importance of right insights:

"To truly create a more sustainable product, it is imperative to be aware of the stages in which the product has the most negative environmental impact to enable the organization to focus on these areas. An LCA offers a clear picture of the environmental impact of a product during its entire life cycle from exploiting resources to production, transport, usage and maintenance, and the end-of-life options of a product. Such analysis is the beginning for innovations in the areas that are genuinely significant regarding environmental impact and enables a company to involve their supply chain based on facts, working towards real sustainable solutions: in the Interface case, focusing on benign and low-carbon solutions in a circular context."

Sustainable information to trigger sustainable behavior

If sustainability information provided leads directly to sustainable behavior, the Monitor role directly pays off in results. A project with direct feedback information to drivers resulting in more sustainable mobility is a successful example of this proven concept.

Niels van Geenhuizen (Global Leader Sustainable Solutions of Arcadis) explains how he — as CSO — analyzed their mobility-related footprint. Based on this footprint, he then developed and introduced direct feedback information that resulted in more sustainable behavior by the group with the highest negative impact: "At Arcadis Netherlands, 55% of CO_2 emissions come from company-car users. We are firmly committed to encouraging these drivers to travel more sustainably by choosing public transport, for example, or scheduling an appointment via video conferencing. We work together with Fynch Mobility to make the car kilometers more sustainable. We started the process with a monthly message to the individual drivers showing their car fuel consumption and how (s)he is 'ranked' compared to the others. This sparked engaged discussions at the coffee machine every month. In addition, the drivers participate in an online training for sustainable and safe driving. The results are positive. After one year, we reduced 4% CO_2, the second year we even reached 9% reduction. In the years after, we expanded this to an overall 'mobility monitor' in which public transport use and air travel was added, developing the tool from CO_2 per car kilometer, to CO_2 per travel kilometer. Currently this data is available in an app on their mobile and, with sustainable choices, they can earn coins to buy sustainable products in a web shop."

Renewable energy — wind for the trains — Monitor role

The Monitor role was crucial in three different ways regarding the wind for the trains; first, to gather the facts and data to be able to exactly specify our energy-use profile to the market parties; second, to gather the data to build a strong business case; and third, to report to our stakeholders the impact of the wind for the trains.

In addition to the annual report, which shows the overall impact of the wind for the trains for society (Figure 8.3), NS also uses other channels to communicate its sustainability performance. It is important that our customers can make a conscious choice and can compare the train to other methods of transportation. This information is shared for example, in the online planning tools for travelers (Figure 8.5) and in screens on the trains. The necessity of solid data — proof that what you are saying is true — has increased over time. Stakeholders, like the media or clients, critically review our data on a regular basis.

For our sustainability performance, it is crucial to be completely transparent about the source of the information, what the underlying assumptions are, and how complete and reliable the information is. Verification by an independent third party can help in that case. For NS, the comparison of CO_2 emissions across

FIGURE 8.5 **NS Journey Planner**

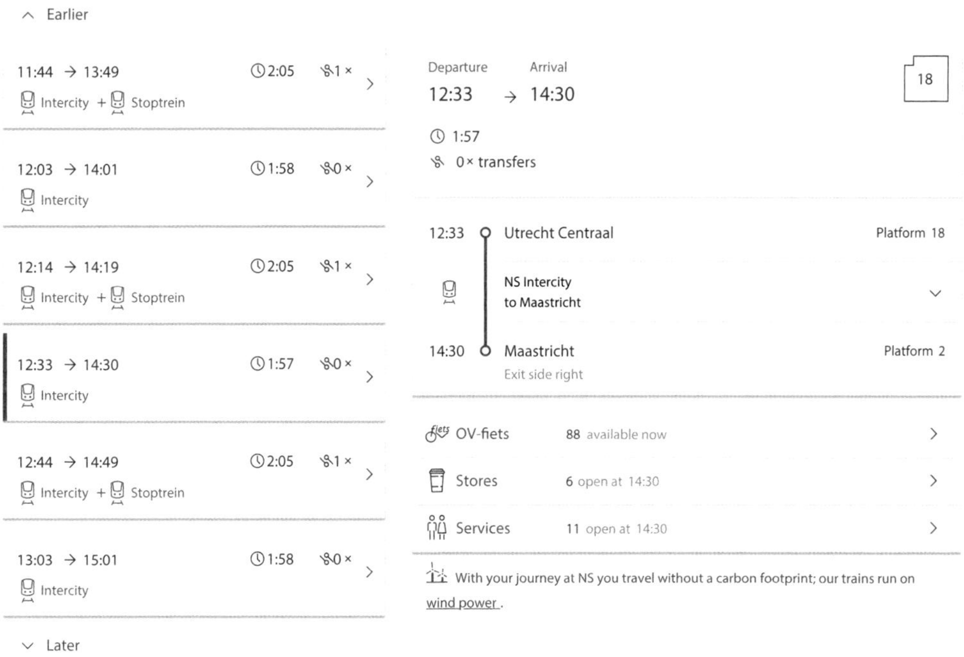

∧ Earlier

11:44 → 13:49	⏱ 2:05	⇄ 1 ×	>
🚈 Intercity + 🚈 Stoptrein			

12:03 → 14:01	⏱ 1:58	⇄ 0 ×	>
🚈 Intercity			

12:14 → 14:19	⏱ 2:05	⇄ 1 ×	>
🚈 Intercity + 🚈 Stoptrein			

12:33 → 14:30	⏱ 1:57	⇄ 0 ×	>
🚈 Intercity			

12:44 → 14:49	⏱ 2:05	⇄ 1 ×	>
🚈 Intercity + 🚈 Stoptrein			

13:03 → 15:01	⏱ 1:58	⇄ 0 ×	>
🚈 Intercity			

∨ Later

Departure	Arrival		18
12:33 →	**14:30**		

⏱ 1:57
⇄ 0 × transfers

12:33	Utrecht Centraal	Platform 18
	NS Intercity to Maastricht	∨
14:30	Maastricht Exit side right	Platform 2

🚲 OV-fiets	88 available now	>
☕ Stores	6 open at 14:30	>
👥 Services	11 open at 14:30	>

🍃 With your journey at NS you travel without a carbon footprint; our trains run on wind power .

different methods of transportation are provided by MilieuCentraal, an independent environmental organization initiated by the Dutch Ministry of Environment. MilieuCentraal is also one of the NGOs that were involved during the entire process of getting our trains to run on wind power.

Tips for Monitors

- Use facts and numbers in communications.
- "A picture says a thousand words", is also very true if it shows sustainability information.
- Make use of third parties to support the credibility of your communications and calculations.
- Realize that beliefs can be strong; if facts and data will not turn the tide, find other solutions.
- Do not use too many indicators or metrics to measure your key performance areas (indicators), select the most material ones.
- For the choice of metrics or indicators, consider:
    - Indicators used in the sector — this can be very useful for benchmarking
    - Indicators from reporting guidelines such as GRI, so they can be used more often and become more relevant
    - Indicators from external agreements to avoid rework or confusion about different indicators for the same topic
    - The availability of company-specific metrics or indicators like production output, from which you can compile relative indicators that take the growth of your business into account.
- Focus on the information required to control, communicate and report in order to achieve your sustainability goals. For example, KPIs in the appraisal system for managers and in quarterly/annual reporting, for appealing (visual) communications or dashboards and information needed for the business case for sustainability or direct feedback to change behavior.
- Align your performance indicators or metrics and baseline measurements with existing reporting requirements as much as possible.
- For the performance indicators or metrics, use existing data collection processes as much as possible.
- Focus on what you should measure, rather than on how to measure it.
- Choose performance indicators or metrics and goals which can be managed.
- Determine who is the owner of the KPI and metrics, how it is calculated and who is the owner of the data processes to measure progress. Document this, for example in a handbook, for which you will also need an owner.
- You manage what you measure, so do not just measure the intended output, but also the impacts.
- Do not just measure within the company, but also in its environment: in the value chain and society. Use an LCA to get a clear picture of the environmental impact of a product during its entire life cycle.
- Do not view ESG reporting guidelines and standards as an instrument for compliance, but rather as a way to further embed sustainability in the management and control systems of the company.

- Use the growing ESG transparency and the opportunities and risks that follow from it to raise boardroom awareness about the strategic relevance of sustainability.
- Focus on "doing good" and leave compliance to the risk manager and internal watchdog.

9

Sustainability dynamics

"It is always the right time to do something good."

MARTIN LUTHER KING (1929-1969), AMERICAN CIVIL RIGHTS LEADER AND CHRISTIAN MINISTER

The structure of this book — one role per chapter linked to typical sustainability activities within that role — may create the impression that the work of a CSO is very static. Of course, that is not the case. To be a successful sustainability professional, you must constantly change roles during your work. Every situation asks for a different mix of roles and activities.

Next to this inside dynamic, there are external sustainability dynamics as well. For a CSO, an important dynamic is the growth in maturity of sustainability. In the different sustainability maturity levels of organizations, some of the 7 Roles are more relevant than others. Also, the size of the sustainability team or the job levels of sustainability professionals in the organization are likely to be different. In general, a small sustainability team headed by a CSO or CSR director, working on a C-level is more suited for a company in the more mature phase, whereas in some companies, sustainability is so integrated that a separate CSO, CSR or sustainability manager does not (or no longer) exist.

Another relevant external dynamic is the development in strategic themes — often determined by geographical, organizational or other contextual factors. Current themes such as climate and energy, circular economy and social themes might evolve or be replaced by other challenges, asking for different skills and knowledge.

It is the task of the CSO to be aware of these dynamics, to reflect regularly and see what is needed to stay connected to the dynamics of the company and society.

Michael Kobori (former VP Sustainability at Levi Strauss & Co.):

"The role of the CSO is viewed by human resources as most like the CEO role given the breath and strategic impact of issues for which we are responsible."

This chapter highlights examples of sustainability dynamics in relation to the role of the CSO. It also gives a sneak preview of the relevance and focus of "the sustainability team of the future". In the next chapter (about competencies), the effect of different strategic themes on the roles and activities of sustainability professionals will be further described.

9.1 Balancing the roles

There are no guidelines on how to divide your time between the different roles. Results of surveys among CSOs, CSR and sustainability managers in the Netherlands (as shown in Figure 9.1) on their actual and desired time spent, highlighted that they would prefer to spend more time as a Strategist and less as a Monitor. And often, according to them, the Coordinator & Initiator role takes up too much of their time. Surprisingly, checks at an international level show the same result: the Strategic role is always favorite, both in relevance and wanting to spend more time in that role, and the Monitor role is often the least favorite. Little appetite for the Monitor role is understandable if (part of) this role is embedded elsewhere in the organization. However, it is my experience that, even when the reporting part of the Monitor role is embedded in the organization, I could only be a credible and successful Strategist if I had all my facts and figures straight. For me, spending more time on numbers and facts as a Monitor eventually led to spending more time as a Strategist.

Level of sustainability maturity
The roles and activities of the CSO, CSR or sustainability manager (or team) change as sustainability is integrated more deeply into the organization. The different phases or levels of sustainability maturity were introduced earlier in the Chapters about the Strategist and Coordinator role. In the latter role, less time is spent when an organization is more mature because sustainability will already be integrated in governance and organizational structures.

FIGURE 9.1 **Balancing act of CSOs, CSR and sustainability managers in the Netherlands in 2019** (Source: State of the Sustainability Profession Survey 2019, Sustainability University Foundation)

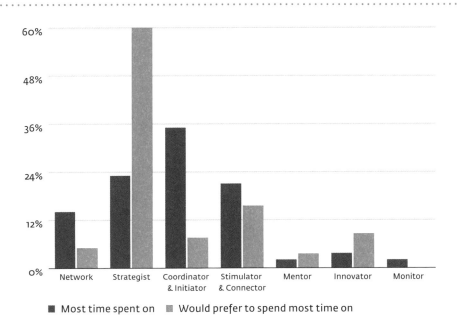

However, other roles are also affected by maturity levels, and each phase has its own "most relevant" roles.

In the starting phase, the CSO, CSR or sustainability manager mostly acts as the Coordinator & Initiator and Stimulator. Time spend as Networker increases and in the next stage, as the Network role matures, more time is spent as the Strategist and Mentor. Then the Innovator role starts to kick in and, over time, the Networker role will be embedded in the organization. All 7 Roles remain important: but the sustainability team will most likely spend less time on them. The Stimulator role transforms more into the Connector, bringing outside in: a role that remains very important. Spending a fair amount of time in your Monitor role is important throughout all phases, since it feeds the other roles. Time spent in this role might increase when a company is in the most mature phase — being a gamechanger in its industries — asking for data to support new business models and investments.

As the level of sustainability knowledge in the organization grows, the need for the Mentor role will decline. Every employee will have to become a sustainability professional to a certain extent. This trend is also supported by the integration of sustainability in many educational programs at

FIGURE 9.2 **Roles and activities of the sustainability team at different levels of sustainability maturity**

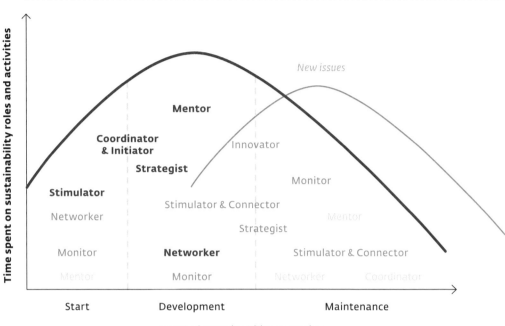

universities and colleges. As stated before, the Coordinator role will also decline over time as sustainability is integrated into systems, processes, and values. Yet in an ever-changing environment, new themes and issues will arise and the time spent in the 7 Roles will intensify and change again; the CSO, CSR or sustainability manager will always retain the role of Coordinator to a certain extent.

Figure 9.2 shows which roles the CSO, CSR or sustainability manager and team spend the most time on at the different maturity levels. The used classification of maturity stages is a simplified version from the model used earlier: from no work on sustainability, sustainability on a project basis, basics of a sustainability program in place, well underway towards full embedding and fully embedded to being an industry game changer.

Some roles decrease in importance. Other roles always remain important but are taken on by other people and departments as sustainability becomes more deeply embedded in the organization. This integration process is greatly enhanced by aligning the sustainability efforts as much as possible with activities, processes and systems that are already in place. As every company is different, what is already in place also varies widely across organizations. For example, if there are no existing relationships with NGOs or other sustainability-related stakeholders, more time will be spent on the tasks of the Networker. Again, there is no "one-size-fits-all". As a CSO, you should be aware of this dynamic and regularly consider if you (and your team) still spend your time in an effective way, aligned with the maturity of sustainability in your company.

Ultimately the integration process is the responsibility of the CSO or sustainability professional. (S)he monitors whether all 7 Roles are properly taken up by others in the business — and intervenes or jumps into whatever role is required.

A mix of roles at the same time

The effectiveness of interventions and activities of a CSO, CSR or sustainability manager always depends on the context in which (s)he is situated. The level of maturity of corporate sustainability integration gives an indication that some roles are more effective or relevant than others for a certain transition period. Regardless of the level of maturity, however, each situation might require another mix of roles at the same time. Other contextual factors such as type of change internal factors such as reorganizations, or external factors such as technological changes might also influence the interventions of a CSO, CSR or sustainability manager. This requires an assessment of a certain context or situation and accordingly, the use of (a mix of) roles, activities and behavior that are considered to be the most effective.

Utrecht and Radboud University, in collaboration with the Dutch National Institute for Public Health and the Environment (Van den Berg et al., 2019[32]), did a study on the internal change agents and their contribution to enhanced corporate sustainability. They concluded that:

1. The success of a change agent is largely determined by contextual factors
2. An effective change agent should be able to act according to a spectrum of worldviews showing elements of several worldviews at the same time.

The power of diversity

In practice it means that a sustainability professional, being such an important formal change agent, must reflect regularly on his or her effectiveness. Does this behavior or activity contribute to successful integration of corporate sustainability? Given the dynamics of the transition process itself, it might well be the case that, over time, because the context is changing, other capabilities are needed to be effective — not only of yourself but also of your team and the more informal change agents in the organizations, such as sustainability ambassadors. The known positive impact of team diversity therefore especially holds for sustainability teams. The CSO can increase team effectiveness by searching for complementary drivers, knowledge, skills and competencies of his or her team members. Eventually you might even have to recruit or look for other people to accelerate the transition to sustainable success.

Balancing the roles with disruptive technologies

The development of disruptive technologies is expected to have an enormous impact on the dynamics of the work and role of the sustainability team of the (near) future. This external factor will change the focus and therefore the balance of the roles and sustainability dynamics.

Darlene Damm (Chair and Principal Faculty of Global Grand Challenges with Singularity University):

> *"In a world with disruptive technologies we should redefine the role of the CSO: from Chief Sustainability Officer, to Corporate Ethical Officer"*

According to Darlene Damm, the role of the CSO or sustainability team in a world with disruptive technologies will change in several ways. The focus will shift to social issues and the Strategist, Network and Innovator roles will increase in relevance.

1 The focus will change in the coming years because:
  - Digitization of the world leads to lower cost and therefore technologies can scale and become more sophisticated. This trend holds for all technologies. That means that Global Goal-driven technologies, such as technologies that aim for "zero hunger", can also scale (for example, Handsfree hectare, IRON ok).
  - Because of the low cost of technologies, the difference between supplying to "wealthy" customers or poor (typically NGO) will diminish (for example, 360ed Myanmar).
  - Therefore, within 10 to 15 years, scarcity will be solved (for example, Regen villages).

To conclude: eventually the environmental problems can/will be solved by disruptive technologies, however a new set of societal problems will arise that the CSO should signal in the Network role such as balance of power (nobody is in power anymore), fake news and privacy.

2   CSO should in his/her Strategic role support the company with its license to grow, based on the new needs of society:

- New business models will arise. Big and very small companies will survive: those in between — probably not.
- In order to survive, a company needs to go back to its DNA (the "why" of its existence) and see what it can do for the needs of society from the perspective of the DNA (for example Japan Airlines — teleportation; and fertilizer — nourishing people).

3   CSO should (in its Network role) seek collaboration to build a sustainable ecosystem for industry.

- It is expected that about forty companies will build all our goods. This can create major opportunities for a circular economy, since the circular economy needs collaboration.
- In the meantime, the future role of the CSO will be about working with other organizations (collaboration) and with regulators. The ecological challenges might be solved by disruptive technologies, leaving ethical issues to be solved by regulators. The CSO will become the Corporate Ethical Officer, since the new sustainability issues will focus on distribution of wealth/equity.

In the Innovator role, the CSO should proactively embed sustainable and ethical criteria in the development of new technology. Darlene expands on this new role of Corporate Ethical Officer: "In general, there are three types of companies: bad, mixed and good companies (such as Patagonia). Especially the second category of 'mixed companies' is in need of redefining the role of a CSO into a Corporate Ethical Officer, because they might have good intentions but have failed to think through the rest of their business model; for example, as 'service' or platform companies with positive environmental benefits but with negative social impacts outside the company. Ethics and/ or risk frameworks (like Omydyar and Ethicalos.org) can support this new role of the CSO, anticipating the future social impact and other risks of technologies."

Balancing the roles in transforming your company in a Doughnut enterprise

While at work, a sustainability professional must constantly change roles in order to be effective. The roles can hardly be seen separately as they often support another role. A great example of this concept was given by Kate Raworth — economist and writer of the book *Doughnut Economics: Seven Ways to Think Like a 21st Century Economist*. During an interview I asked her, what can a CSO do to transform a company into a "Doughnut enterprise" — a company whose core business activity helps to meet the needs of all, within the means of the planet? While riding together in a train fueled by wind power in the

Netherlands, she not only answered that question but also showed me how the other 6 Roles are needed to be effective as a Strategist.

In order to become a Doughnut enterprise — and to deliver generative results[33] — Kate Raworth states that companies can only do so if they align all five of these business design traits: purpose, governance, networks, ownership and finance(Figure 9.3).[34]

FIGURE 9.3 **Doughnut Economy (Kate Raworth)**

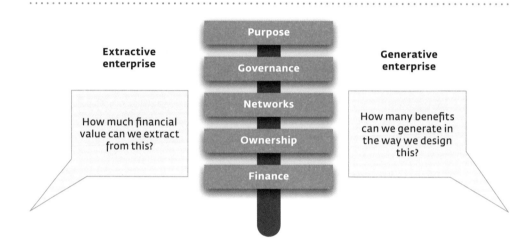

The CSO can be key in transforming a company into becoming a Doughnut enterprise, especially in (re)defining its purpose (Strategist role) which is key, finding aligned partners (Networker role) and aligning governance (Monitor role) by setting long-term Doughnut metrics. However, once the enterprise has changed its strategy into "being generative", all 7 Roles are important in implementing it (roles of Stimulator, Coordinator, Innovator and Mentor). What is not mentioned here are the two toughest design criteria — ownership and finance. It may not be easy for the CSO to influence ownership but he/she can certainly influence the relationship with finance; for example, in terms of making his or her company a leader on carbon disclosure.

Kate Raworth: "In order to be able to fulfil your role as Strategist (lead for strategy/purpose) you should be in the right position. Who are you seen as (a CSO)? A great indicator is: where do you report to? Where are you in the organization and how serious is your role taken? A CSO should report to the board and not to staff directors of legal, finance or communication departments. The next thing is to figure out a way to get The Doughnut into the boardroom. Before you even can think about incorporating Doughnut thinking into your strategy/purpose, you have to open up the conversation in the boardroom (Stimulator & Connector role). You could use visuals and/or gaming to answer the central question: how do we contribute? Do we have impact and/or how does this affect us? The open discussion will change the mindset of the board. In addition, a great way to shift mindsets is to show what the competition does. As a CSO, you probably have a great network (Networker) and can share the best practices of 'competing' companies/partners, with values that you want your board to embrace.

The strategy could be set by plotting where you are in The Doughnut currently and where you would like to be in three or five years. To support implementation of a Doughnut strategy (Coordinator & Initiator role), it helps to show a good business case and this effect should be supported by data (Monitor role). To give an example, there is a great business case for the human resource department. Implementing a Doughnut strategy and purpose will attract and motivate the current and especially the next generation employees. In addition, if employees are motivated by heart, they bring in their full selves to the job, facilitating the CSO's Mentor role: empower others for success. To achieve the set goals, circular/Doughnut criteria should be set for designing innovations. The CSO as Innovator can support defining those criteria."

9.2 Sustainability dynamics in practice

Balancing the 7 Roles in a global environment

According to Wineke Haagsma (Director Corporate Sustainability PwC The Netherlands & EMEA) the 7 Roles of a CSO, CSR or sustainability manager are broadly and globally recognized. Answering the question about which mix of roles is most effective in a global environment, she tells that this greatly depends on three things: timing, culture and stakeholders.

"For timing, you need to analyze at which stage of maturity is sustainability in your organization. Then be sensitive to the particular culture you are working in. Different roles are more effective in certain regions than in others, all depending on the culture. Last but not least, your stakeholders: everyone has a personal preference in style and the way you approach them and bring them on board. Only if you make a sharp analysis on those three, will you be able to find the right mix of roles that optimize your sustainable transition."

Sustainability dynamics in Africa

Since 2007, Dr Franck Eba — as a CSO — built, structured and coordinated the sustainable development approach of the SIFCA group in agro-industry and more specifically in the oilseeds, rubber and sugar sectors: a group approach implemented in ten companies in West Africa. SIFCA specialized in "African CSR", which takes into account the realities of the countries, regions and sites where they operate by setting realistic objectives. For seven years, through responsibility, behaviour was changed, rates of workplace accidents reduced, rates of infectious diseases such as malaria and AIDS were reduced, excellence and education fostered, and the environmental footprint reduced.

In his Network role, he is campaigning African CSR, communicating in various forums and seminars in Europe and Africa by affirming a true African identity. With measured and realistic ambitions and focusing on operationality and returning experience (when it comes to education and training), the awareness and dissemination of the CSR concept in Côte d'Ivoire and Africa have gained momentum. This promotion of African CSR especially adapted to local realities could be a real lever for sustainable development in Africa. In that way, CSR would be formalized and extended to other companies and organizations.

> *"To support this development, it is necessary to capitalize and share the good examples of private groups and also the good state models such as Rwanda and Ghana."*

Advantages of CSR for a company in Africa are the same as for other companies, such as reputation, efficiency gains, a more sustainable organization; however, they still are often misunderstood. Constraints like a poor understanding of the CSR concept, often referred to as the "thing of the rich", poverty, family pressure, costs for environmental and social compliance, lack of governance, legal framework or local expertise and lack of incentives or management involvement, are all elements that hinder the CSR "wave" in Africa.

Organizing African CSR

Franck Eba explains how CSR and his CSO role is organized. SIFCA is a holding group organization. The CSO is responsible for implementing the CSR group process in five countries and seven subsidiaries in West Africa (30,000 workers). During his years as CSO, he elaborated the CSR strategy and implemented it. Also, as the CSO, he was in charge of reporting and communication.

At SIFCA, CSR is organized with focal points in each subsidiary, (CSR managers, HR managers, QSE managers, social/stakeholder managers): in total, about twenty-five managers (some top managers). Additionally, there was a CSR team in the holding consisting of an environmental manager, social and stakeholder relation manager, safety manager, and a reporting manager. Part of the Coordinator role of the CSO was creating this network and introducing CSR indicators in managers' evaluations to push them to get involved. As a good example, Franck Eba (in the Stimulator role) invited workers to communicate in meetings and seminars and he supported campaigns and training to raise awareness. With the CSR information from his Monitor role, he regularly communicated with the Executive Group Board, creating a sense of competition by showing goals and results in CSR.

> *"I was reporting to the CEO group of the Holding. This helped me to push CEOs of subsidiaries to make their contribution to the CSR strategy. I was also pushed and supported by my mentor, the CEO of the group (Yves Lambelin), working with me on the ground and completely engaged until, in 2011, he was tragically killed in our civil war."*

Experienced keys to success of implementing a CSR strategy at SIFCA were:
- Including an African approach in the CSR strategy that takes into account local realities
- Favourable commodity prices that have generated profits and therefore CSR budgets
- Shareholder and donor confidence in financing
- The strong involvement and vision of top management
- The lasting relationship with planters sealed by a win-win partnership
- An openness to excellence and innovation with CDM (Clean Development Mechanisms) projects, generating carbon credits through the production of green energy and green building projects in stabilized earth bricks
- Strategic and technical partnerships with organizations involved in CSR (Michelin, OIPR, IECD, ACONDA, etc.).

Reinforcing results that supported implementation were:
- Economic (financial) benefits such as the realized improvements of the existing sustainable production models in the agro-industry
- The perceived attractiveness (reputational capital) of incorporating social responsibility in the company
- Feelings of belonging, attractive for workers.

Balancing the 7 Roles in Africa

Franck Eba recognizes using all 7 Roles to reach his goals; however, the informal roles such as the Networker and Stimulator role and the use of interpersonal skills were most dominant and crucial. Below, Franck explains in his own words, his view on the CSO role in Africa:

"I had to be diplomatic and take into account the cultural reality of the different areas. For example, in the north of Côte d'Ivoire, women were not allowed to discuss the development of local communities, impacted by our company activities. First, I was obliged to discuss the development of local communities without the women. Finally, I succeeded in convincing them to let me have discussions with these women to find out how I could support them.

Culture, religions, traditions and African beliefs are our reality. We have to consider all of this in the CSR strategy and do the job step by step. That is why I talk about African CSR, which is not the same as (a) European or a rich country's CSR. How can you convince people to protect rare animals in the forest when they do not have enough food to eat? How can you implement good governance in a region where corruption is everywhere? How can you convince labor workers not to use children when they ask you: 'If they do not work who will give them food? How will they eat? They do not work they do not eat!'

I was confronted by such situations on the ground. CSR is not in the offices with beautiful clothes and air-condition(ing). It is in the place, deep in people, deep in their realities.

You have to create your own indicators (that do not exist in GRI), from your reality. Just to give you the example of voluntary people who carry out the HIV test... How many children have we saved by our awareness campaigns...? The successes in school. You have to create your CSR world!

A CSO is a transversal job, with skills and knowledge of many fields. Personally, I have done a lot of auditor's certificates. You have to be ready all the time for training, and learning to adapt to your role. You have to be open and must be able to convince people to change as you have changed already. They must recognize themselves in you. I had to be a good communicator, passionate, engaged, concrete and real. But most of all I had to be a model, an ambassador, simple, respect the traditions, respect the people, and be accessible!"

9.3 The sustainability team of the future

In the end, when sustainable success has transformed your company into an industry game changer and the rules of the game are based on sustainable principles, what remains of the sustainability team? If all roles are embedded, what else does the organization need? What is your added value as the CSR or CSO manager at that stage?

What remains is the need to keep challenging the organization. With leadership skills, the sustainability professional will continue to connect people and ideas and urge the organization to raise the bar, matching the changing needs of society. Signaling relevant external (sustainability) trends and connecting these to the company through a multidisciplinary and holistic vision. All companies need someone to detect such outside developments, which may translate into threats or opportunities for the company. Integrating part of the Innovator role in the Stimulator role, with knowledge of the company, its processes and systems, the CSO, CSR or sustainability manager is well placed to fulfill this role. Some argue that this ultimately is the role of the CEO. The question is whether the long-term focus and external orientation of this role will have to compete too much with the CEO's other priorities. The future will tell whether this role stays with the sustainability manager or CSO, or might be taken up by the CEO of the future.

Redundancy at last?

So, should CSOs, CSR and sustainability managers strive to make themselves redundant or continue at full power? "Both," says André Veneman, former Corporate Director Sustainability of AkzoNobel on this question, "CSR managers are catalysts, starters and change agents. The art of the CSR manager is to be a coach who helps every business unit, every position and ultimately every employee to take responsibility for the sustainability strategy. As soon as a business unit or function, such as purchasing, supply chain, research, sales and marketing or human resources, has embedded the sustainability strategy in its daily business operations, we are — temporarily — superfluous. When does our role stop? Never. The challenges are unbelievably large, the transition paths to a circular economy and to social cohesion are long, fundamental changes are needed in business development, new partnerships and public-private financing. We are only at the beginning of that transition."

According to Venema, all companies need "outside-in thinkers", "analytical, critical and creative minds". People who translate the longer term into concrete short-term objectives. People who know how to inspire, do and accelerate. We are moving from awareness to accelerate and action: the CSR manager is only at the start of this race.

Jacobine Das Gupta, Director Sustainability at DSM agrees with Venema, that the job of a CSO is "here to stay": "Sustainability will, sooner or later, become part of most business functions. As companies start to articulate their societal 'purpose' or 'missions' alongside business objectives, the yardsticks and interventions will be embedded in a range of functions like strategy, finance, innovation, marketing, sales and sourcing. Sustainability will help to provide a compass for doing the right thing while doing business. It is, however, unlikely that the sustainability discipline will disappear completely within the next few years. Like safety health and environment (SHE), quality management, supply chain management, the métier is likely to further develop and here to stay. Perhaps we will call it something else and maybe there will be multiple spin-off functions — but a central strategic, antenna, and supporting role is likely here to stay. I think we can look forward to a future of 'Corporate Climate Warriors' and 'Chief Happiness Officers' who will help take business to a new level."

Sustainability competencies

"The future depends on what you are doing right now."

MAHATMA GANDHI

What competencies does a CSO need to be effective? Competencies — or the ability to perform effectively in a certain type of task or problem situation — are closely related to what we expect of someone in terms of attitude and behavior. So, sustainability competencies are — in behavior — an observable combination of the knowledge, skills, attitude and personal qualities that we expect of an effective sustainability professional. These specific personal characteristics, reflected in effective behavior, can relate to many different things, like whether you take decisions quickly or would rather take some more time to get further insights. Both of these characteristics are neither positive nor negative, but they are more useful in some roles than in others.

Competencies can express themselves in behavior but there are also less visible sides to them, like personal characteristics. In principle, you can develop any competency — unlike a talent — by learning and practice. But the more closely the competency is related to your personality, such as the ability to self-reflect or be openminded, the more challenging it will be to develop it.

Next to an introduction to the 8 sustainability competencies, this chapter highlights the difference in perceived importance of roles and competencies of sustainability professionals, with different strategic sustainability themes. And it shows the first findings of a known job-classification framework applied to different job levels of the sustainability profession, from sustainability project manager to CSO.

10.1 **The CSR competency framework**

Scientific research on the competencies of CSR and CSO managers[35] differentiates 8 competencies. These are divided into four kinds: cognition, functional, social and meta-oriented competencies, as shown in Figure 10.1. The next section of this chapter outlines how these competencies are relevant to each of the roles of the CSR or CSO manager.

Many experienced CSR and CSO managers agree that what you need to be effective in any organization when working on sustainability is a deep understanding of the company, an internal network across functions and a good understanding of different disciplines. You never work from just one discipline, but across functions, ranging from the supply chain, marketing, sales, public affairs and communications to R&D. Only then you will be able to identify risks and opportunities, to create connections, to build bridges. In addition, you will need a robust understanding of sustainability, otherwise you will not understand what it is all about, and you cannot be a serious partner in the dialogue with NGOs and other stakeholders.

FIGURE 10.1 **Competencies of the CSR manager or professional**

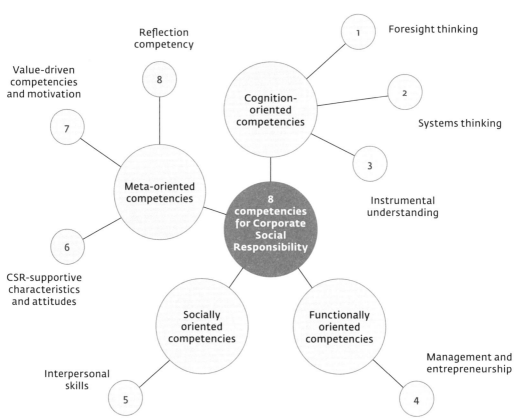

Cognition-oriented competencies

1 *Foresight thinking*: anticipating future developments regarding CSR-related challenges for the company.	The ability to think in scenarios, to anticipate and to critically assess. Bring the outside in.
2 *Systems thinking*: understanding the interdependency between systems and subsystems that are relevant for CSR. Ability to think holistically.	Visualization, understanding and analysis of complex, dynamic systems and issues, both externally (for example, in the value chain) and internally (for example, how the company runs). Insight into corporate processes and the underlying connections. Knowledge of systems inside and outside of the company. Knowledge of that which needs to be done to change systems.
3 *Instrumental understanding*: understanding CSR-relevant drivers, values, standards and regulations.	Ability to understand and deal with regulation, politics, governance and standards at the sector, national or international level. Contribute to the development of instruments. Also, the ability to understand the underlying intrinsic drivers of corporate sustainability.

Functionally oriented competencies

4 *Management and entrepreneurship*: managing or leading CSR and identifying, prioritizing and realizing CSR-related business opportunities.	Ability to develop a sustainability vision and to translate this into a sustainability program/plan, as well as manage it. Entrepreneurial skills to be able to see and realize opportunities. Ability to create a business case and to know the company well enough to be able to drive decisions and implementation. Change and program management skills, such as: ● Ability to deal with a changing context, while holding on to your own goals ● Creating a sense of urgency for long-term issues in a short-term environment ● The ability to make choices and prioritize in the context of what is relevant for the organization.

Socially oriented competencies

5 *Interpersonal skills*: realizing CSR-supportive interpersonal processes in CSR implementation	Effective social, communicative and networking skills. Flexibility in styles, ability to adjust yourself to the other person and situation. Creating awareness and ownership for sustainability with others. Coaching and supporting others to integrate sustainability into their daily tasks. Ability to motivate, facilitate and stimulate collaboration in the area of sustainability. Ability to identify stakeholders. Ability to work in multidisciplinary and multicultural partnerships, simultaneously serving both the company's needs and stakeholder interests.

Meta-oriented competencies

6 CSR-supportive characteristics and attitudes	Sustainability professionals are ethical, empathetic, committed, enthusiastic, creative, open-minded, flexible, patient, persistent and pragmatic in their approach. They are able to inspire others and to put the interests of others above their own (ego).
7 Value-driven competencies and motivation	A high sense of urgency and intrinsic motivating to act on sustainability challenges. Finding a balance between idealism and pragmatism. Consistency in "what you stand for","what you say" and "what you do".
8 Reflection competency	Ability to challenge your own ideas, habits, and assumptions and to act upon this. Self-reflection and self-evaluation ability.

As Anniek Mauser (Unilever) puts it:

"You can definitely grow in the job, but it is often underestimated how important both corporate and sustainability knowledge is for success. Companies should consider a sustainability career track, to ensure people who are suitable for the role get cross-functional experience."

10.2 Competencies for each role

The Networker

To be an effective Networker, you need social, communicative and networking skills. You build networks and facilitate collaboration on sustainability topics. You need to be able to identify stakeholders and be able to work in multidisciplinary and multicultural teams in order to serve the interests of both the company and the stakeholders. A good Networker needs *management and entrepreneurship* competencies as well as *interpersonal skills*. You are a good listener, you embrace diversity as well as the different disciplines of the different internal and external stakeholders. You will also benefit from more personal meta-competencies such as the ability to *reflect* on your own sustainability perspectives and experiences to learn from your peers. Finally, *systems thinking* is important to establish which stakeholders provide an opportunity for joint sustainable value creation.

The Strategist

The core responsibility of the Strategist is to think and operate at the strategic level. The key competencies for the Strategist are *systems thinking, management and entrepreneurship*. You need to know how systems function within and outside of the organization and what is needed to make systems sustainable. You also need to be able to deal with a changing context and yet maintain focus on your own goals. *Interpersonal skills* and *foresight thinking* also support the Strategist in the boardroom. Outside-the-box thinking is also important for this role but. if that is not your forte, you can always engage people with that skill.

The Coordinator & Initiator

Translating the sustainability vision and mission to the organization requires many competencies. You need *systems thinking* to understand the relevant systems and sub-systems, including any mutual interdependencies and what is needed to change these systems. You need knowledge and insight into how the organization is structured and led, to be able to translate sustainability into the company's strategic plan, structures and systems and to *manage* the organization of sustainability accordingly. *Interpersonal skills* are key to drive change without hierarchical power. Last but not least, you need *management and entrepreneurial* skills to be able to seize opportunities, initiate projects, activities and to manage change.

The Stimulator & Connector

To generate support, a sustainability professional needs both content knowledge and *interpersonal skills*. The content knowledge is needed to be able to align with different disciplines and to create connections. So, *systems thinking* is important in this role as well. *Instrumental thinking*, for example the ability to understand the underlying intrinsic drivers of corporate sustainabiliy is also required. The *interpersonal skills* needed include effective social, communicative and networking skills, such as adjusting your style to different situations, communicating with different people in different roles like a chameleon. The role also requires the ability to listen actively and to ask probing questions. The sustainability professional also needs to confirm the positive self-image of others, avoiding letting his/her own ego getting in the way supplemented with relevant CSR *support characteristics*, such as creativity, and *intrinsic motivation* to inspire others.

The Mentor

Only through multidisciplinary knowledge can you create a relevant translation of sustainability for each department and role from the context in which the company operates. This requires the ability to think holistically. *Instrumental understanding* is needed to work with specific functions such as finance. Project *management* is needed to be able to structurally advise, inform and train people so they can achieve their sustainability tasks and goals. As most professionals know best how to integrate sustainability into their job, this also requires *interpersonal skills* to empower people to initiative sustainable activities within the context of their own role. This might sound easy, but it requires a strong dose of CSR *supporting personal characteristics* such as empathy, patience and persistence.

The Innovator

For the Innovator, the ability to think outside the box is really important. You need to be creative and open-minded and to challenge yourself and others — and to let others challenge and surprise you. *Reflection* is important, as is a willingness to make mistakes and the ability to learn from them. Holistic *systems thinking* is needed to enter into unexpected and innovative alliances. The Innovator needs to think ahead, using *foresight thinking* to be able to bring future developments from the outside into the organization. As well as *interpersonal skills*, do not let all the reasons "why not" prevent you from making progress, but let yourself be the one asking "why not"?

The Monitor

Instrumental thinking and analytical capabilities are very important for the Monitor. The analytical skills are part of the sustainability management competency, using relevant information to lead to the desired decision-making and, if needed, developing additional financial skills; for example, structured consideration of the best metrics to help integrate sustainability, to report on progress and to make the results relevant for external and internal stakeholders. *Systems thinking* is also an important competency, to be able to translate non-financial values to financial ones, enabling integrated decision-making.

The level of sustainability competency we expect from an effective sustainability professional will depend on the type of job. The *systems thinking* skills of a CSO in a multinational requires a different combination of knowledge, skills, attitude and personal qualities than the *systems thinking* skills of a sustainability team member.

10.3 Leveraging competencies in practice

Although sustainability competencies are needed for the 7 Roles, the question remains, however, as to how specific these competencies are for the sustainability professional in comparison with other professions. The same holds for the profession itself. How different is the profession of a CSO from a change or program manager? Although more research is needed to answer these questions, practice shows that it is especially the need for flexibility in styles and combination of competencies to adjust to every situation that distinguishes the dynamic multidisciplinary "leadership by influence" role of a CSO or CSR from other managers. However, the transitions we are facing might require these types of competencies in other professions as well.

Competencies related to circular economy and climate & energy transitions

First results of the research on "circular economy competencies" of CSOs, CSR and sustainability managers conducted by Sustainability University Foundation and supported by the Goldschmeding Foundation, show that, to be effective in the field of circular economy, different competencies are important when compared with competencies in the field of climate and energy transition (Figure 10.2).

Although systems thinking, forward thinking and management and entrepreneurship were — for both transitions — effective competencies, in the opinion of CSOs, CSR and sustainability managers in the Netherlands, systems thinking is the number one most important competency for circular economy and foresight thinking in the case of climate and energy transition.

FIGURE 10.2 **Most important competency according to sustainability professionals**
(Source: SOP survey 2019, Sustainability University Foundation supported by The Goldschmeding Foundation)

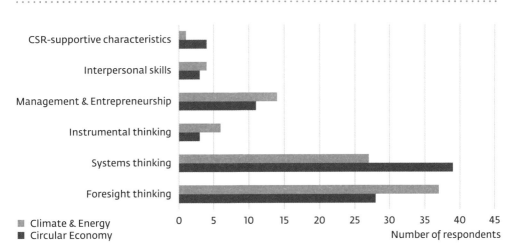

Remarkably, the same roles — Strategist, Coordinator and Stimulator — are considered to be the most important for both transitions, which might support the idea that roles are more dependent on the maturity of sustainability in an organization. However, the Innovator Role was mentioned more frequently as most important role in relation to Circular Economy than Climate & Energy.

It is recognized by leading CSOs, CSR and sustainability managers that working in the field of circular economy requires a different set of skills to be effective than is usually available in companies. Sustainability professionals in companies are responsible for transforming their business into climate-neutral, circular and inclusive companies. Although the climate and energy transition also asks companies for radically different strategies (drawing on analytical competencies such as foresight thinking), the transition itself can be done involving a relatively small number of people in the company, value chain and stakeholders. Circular-economy projects, however, ask for a complete transformation of all business processes and influence the core of company strategies. It is, therefore, more complex and requires cooperation with many people, inside and outside the company.

Circular economy requires system thinking or "structured transformation thinking": what will our circular business model look like and how can we transform our business into this model? You really have to understand and know the core of your different business activities, products and supply chains to understand what the problem and the solution might be.

"Circular economy (CE) is unique because it links products to business models. A circular goal cannot be achieved only with the engineering and design of a product; all other disciplines need to be involved, such as procurement, finance, marketing and even sales. CE only works if you do it together, all at the same time."

EELCO SMIT — SENIOR DIRECTOR SUSTAINABILITY — GROUP
SUSTAINABILITY, PHILIPS INTERNATIONAL B.V.

As a CSO, CSR or sustainability manager you can only achieve your circular goals if you proactively involve the various businesses in the value chain and show that they can benefit from the new circular business model. This requires the skills to engage all relevant multidisciplinary partners with an understanding of your business, the value chain and the underlying business models.

An effective way to start a circular project is to organize a multidisciplinary workshop focusing on the value proposition for the customer and the contribution to that value by every discipline in the value chain, such as manufacturer and repairer. It is often a puzzle to find a way that every discipline will both add to the circular model and gets its share of the circular business pie. A CSO, CSR or sustainability manager should like these complex puzzles of making a circular business case and have a basic knowledge of design and materials. Finding answers to the two main questions: how do we close the loop? (how will we get our products back after use?) and how do we make a circular design? require all these skills.

"You cannot work in the field of circular economy from behind your desk: you have to proactively engage all relevant partners in the value chain. To better understand the complexity (and opportunities), it certainly helps if you have worked in different relevant functions in your company."

JEROEN COX — SENIOR MANAGER ENERGY & ENVIRONMENT KPN

In the end, the "goodwill factor" is also an important condition for being effective. In general, goodwill increases when the CSO, CSR or sustainability manager can show that working with a circular business model benefits the company, customer and the planet. When the CSO, CSR or sustainability manager — as a professional — also shows personal commitment to, and passion for, the company and its product, the "goodwill factor" increases further.

Sustainable job classification

Sustainability/CSR professional is a broad term and covers the whole range from the youngest team member in the sustainability team up to the CSO. At stakeholder, organizational, team and individual level, everyone has his or her own role and responsibility, horizontally as well as vertically, connecting these different levels.

According to the often-used (open) Hay method, 4 levels of jobs classifications for CSOs, CSR and sustainability managers can be identified:

1 Chief Sustainability Officer (in a multinational)
2 CSR director/Chief Sustainability Officer (of a national organization or a division or country of a multinational)
3 Sustainability/CSR project manager
4 Team member in a sustainability team.

These four levels differ significantly in know-how, problem-solving and accountability, justifying a separate level (as shown in Figure 10.3). A Chief Sustainability Officer, being part of the so-called C-suite of an organization, is able to act at executive level and to participate in general business discussions beyond the scope of sustainability. Typically, level 1 CSOs work for multinational companies that are able to create a sustainable system change in its market or supply chain. This CSO, working on a multinational level, is accountable for the development of the integrated sustainable strategy and related business models, whereas the level 2 CSO of a national organization, division or country is typically accountable for:

- Developing programs and projects to integrate the "headquarters" strategy and goals within the division or country for which (s)he is working
- Development of the integrated sustainable strategy for a national/regional company with relatively little influence to change "the rules of the game".

Both levels of CSO jobs develop relevant networks to achieve their goals.

The CSR project managers (level 3):

- Usually report to the CSO director or manager
- Operate at a more tactical level or strategic for a local operating company, and
- Are accountable for the realization of projects or work/initiatives that support corporate sustainability integration.

FIGURE 10.3 **Example of job classification sustainability managers**

Level 1	Level 2	Level 3	Level 4
Chief Sustainability Officer (CSO)	Sustainability/CSR Director (manager) Chief Sustainability Officer	Sustainability or CSR project manager	Team member in a sustainability team
Role overview			
• C-suite multinational • Strategic level (system change business models)	• Board national organization or a division/country of a multinational • Strategic/tactical level	• Reporting to CSO or manager • Local operating company • Tactical/operational level	• Reporting to manager • Operational level • No managerial duties
Know-how			
• In-depth knowledge of the working of large and complex organizations • General managerial & leadership skills • Business and systems development • Highly advanced sustainability competencies (expert level)	• In-depth knowledge of the working of organizations • Broad relevant experience and managerial skills • Academic/applied science background • Advanced sustainability competencies (senior/expert	• Knowledge of the working of organizations • Sustainability competencies (senior level) • Academic/applied science background • Managerial skills	• Knowledge of the working of organizations • Sustainability competencies (junior level) • Applied science background
Problem-solving			
• Self-defined/long-term strategy • International company playing field • Very high degree of uncertainty	• Within defined strategy • National, part of international company playing field • High degree of uncertainty	• Within defined strategy and framework • National/local company playing field • Above-average degree of uncertainty	• Within defined goals • Part of company playing field • Certain degree of uncertainty
Accountability			
• Development and integration CSR strategy and business models (& network) • Authority to act within company governance/policy • Part of profit (indirect)	• Realization of CSR strategy and CSR integration (& network) • Authority to act within strategy • Part of profit (indirect)	• Integration of CSR and realization of CSR projects • Authority to act within strategic framework or goals • Small part of profit (indirect)	• Contribution to integration of CSR and CSR projects realization • Limited authority to act within goals • Very small part of profit (indirect)

CSR or sustainability project or team members (level 4) usually operate on an operational level and have no managerial duties.

In addition to these general sustainability jobs, more CSOs recognize the increasing importance of highly specialized and technical skills of sustainability professionals, such as the field of water, biodiversity and circular economy. This allows for career advancement as an expert or specialist, rather than a generalist. Such a specialist role could act at a "high level", reporting directly to the CSO or board of a business unit dealing with this specific theme.

"My tip for young professionals who want to work in the field of corporate sustainability is that they should become experts in something such as energy or water. They should bring some technical insights to their role in order to be able to come up with real solutions or innovations."

BRIAN JANOUS (GENERAL MANAGER OF ENERGY AND SUSTAINABILITY AT MICROSOFT)

Brian explains: "The role and competencies of a CSO are growing and becoming more demanding. Historically, these positions were occupied by professionals with a communications background or project managers. However, these positions will more and more be filled by scientist and environmentalists. As a CSO, you should be able to speak the language of the people of your company. This means — for a tech company — that you need to have technical skills and an understanding of how you could integrate sustainability into practice."

Remuneration

Job classifications differ from job descriptions, roles and competencies. Job classifications are the criteria by which a job is graded. This is done with a system that objectively and accurately defines and evaluates the duties, responsibilities, tasks, and authority level of a job. In many organizations, the results of a formal job classification is used in job grading and job evaluations to determine what salary a given position deserves and to explain the different salary levels for different positions within a company. Often only a selected number of jobs within a company are subjected to classification: all other jobs are graded by plotting similar jobs to those considered equal in terms of know-how, problem-solving and accountability. This so-called relative salary position, therefore, effects the salary of the sustainability professional.

The actual level of remuneration, however, also depends on the business sector and country or region that the CSO, CSR or sustainability manager is working in. So, the same outcome of a job classification can lead to different salaries in different companies or business sectors.

For the human resources departments, sustainability jobs are often difficult to understand and therefore difficult to grade. The jobs are often new, with a broad scope, and a large informal cross-functional influence in organizational authority. Sustainability professionals should be aware of the job-classification system, processes and "language" in their company, to assess whether it might be an opportunity for them to have their job graded. It might also take some time and effort since, for human resource officers, sustainability positions are (still) difficult to rank.

Career opportunities

Career opportunities for the sustainability professionals are many. Over the years, CSOs, CSR and sustainability managers have moved "up", "around" and "out" of the sustainability profession:

- *Moving up*: from team member to sustainability project manager and ultimately, overall responsibility for sustainability in an organization
- *Moving around*: CSO, CSR or sustainability manager in a different business sector with completely different sustainability themes
- *Moving out*: might seem a strange career step for a CSO, CSR or sustainability manager who is intrinsically motivated to transform the business into a sustainable one; but, for the professional development of the individual it might be a good career switch and sometimes your impact is bigger in the business itself than as a CSO, CSR or sustainability manager. Coming back to a corporate sustainability role, it will certainly smooth your career path to have worked in other business functions for a few years.

Ten years ago, when I created my own position as a CSO, this was common practice. Most sustainability roles still had to be created, and companies often placed someone in the CSO role from inside the organization who had good connections across the firm. However, in recent years, a large increase in hiring from outside the company has occurred and the number of jobs is growing. It is part of the development or "professionalization" of sustainability jobs and, since this development is still going on, it might continue to "upgrade" the profession itself and career opportunities.

Personal mix of competencies — wind for the trains

Not all CSR and CSO managers will master all 8 competencies at a senior level. As a result, some of the roles will feel much more natural than others. Yet the other roles have to be delivered as well. It is hard work putting all this into practice. To get wind power for the trains, the competencies, "foresight thinking, systems thinking and management and entrepreneurship", were especially vital. To give an example of the use of foresight thinking in this particular project: anticipating that biomass would not be a sustainable solution for renewable energy in the long run turned out to be a very valuable starting point. At the time, biomass was commonly accepted as a fuel for green energy, even when used as co-fuel in coal-fired plants.

Fortunately, the other most-needed competencies were also present, with my team and myself. Systems thinking and entrepreneurship are frequently used for our circular programs, when harvesting trains for reuse of materials and finding or creating new business around it. When it comes to the other competencies, there is definitely room for improvement however, especially in the more meta-oriented competencies. To speak for myself, I am not always as patient as I should be, my behavior is not always consistent, and I do not take nearly enough time to reflect.

Of the many roles of a CSR or CSO manager, the Stimulator and Innovator fit me best. They provide me with the energy I need and enable me to influence the societal value creation of the company in a positive, opportunity-focused way. I think these are exactly the roles that make the difference in creating the success of wind power for the trains. However, without the others roles that also suit me, but do not give me as much fun and energy — the end might not have worked out so well or had such an impact.

It took about four years of preparations to realize the wind power for the trains, and I had used or organized all 7 Roles and 8 competencies. During the project, I worked on my reflection competency, assessing the effectiveness of our work, roles and activities and the time spent. When needed, I would organize team diversity or develop other roles, skills or competencies, to make sure that we would create sustainable success!

Listen up

How do you keep yourself fit and sane as sustainability professional? Roles, activities, competencies — the CSO or CSR manager is the person dealing with all of this every day. As reasons for work motivation might differ, so can different work situations be reasons for frustration. To be effective, it is important to feel balanced and capable of doing the job and your intuition is an important source of information. When you are fit and balanced, you are better able to listen to this source. When you feel good about yourself in the role, you are more receptive to the other's situation and you are better able to see and hear what the other person or the situation requires.

"When you talk, you often repeat what you already know. When you listen, you often learn something new."

DALAI LAMA

So how do you take care of your own sanity in this role? That is probably quite different from person to person. For inspiration, here are the insights from Nic Marks's TED talk on happiness, five things to do every day to be happy:

1. Connect: be social, get out there and enjoy the company of others
2. Get Active: an obvious one but exercise makes you feel better
3. Take Notice: be aware of what is going on around you, people, the changing seasons, etc.
4. Keep Learning: not necessarily in the formal sense but stay curious
5. Give: it is proven that people who give to others are happier.

As in Shawn Anchor's book, *The Happiness Advantage*, Nic Marks's insights are supported by research on positive psychology. All of these can easily be applied in the different roles of the CSO, CSR or sustainability manager, to provide not only joy in what you do, but also the energy needed to keep going to create sustainable success.

Closing note and prelude to new beginnings

In this book I describe — based on the experiences of many sustainability professionals and scientific research — what it takes to be an effective CSO or CSR manager. It is an evolving, relatively new profession, but 7 Roles, accompanied with the right set of the 8 competencies, are globally seen as key to realizing sustainable transitions in business. Every interview, publication or practical experience gives a new insight and is a lesson learned: how to get things done, to close the gap between sustainable strategies, not to mention the actual implementation. I could keep on writing and rewriting *7 Roles*, and the only reason I write this closing note is because I know that, once *7 Roles* is published, it can also be the first chapter of Creating Sustainable Success for a sustainability professional, somewhere in this world.

Really, I am saying "this is version 1.0" in the hope that you will take "its ingredients" further and develop your own successful recipe — Creating Sustainable Success in your business.

I would like to conclude by sharing a few last remarks that came to my mind when writing *7 Roles*.

It is time to shift the focus to people

The book largely focuses on sustainability professionals, because they are formally appointed to Create Sustainable Success. But what about the other change agents in key business processes, such as finance, procurement, HR or operations? What does it take to make them effective? The CSO, CSR or sustainability manager cannot do it alone. Part of the assignment of a CSO is therefore to also assess if there are sufficient — not formally "appointed" — change agents with the right competencies in the organization to support and sustain the transition. Educating and training (part of) the (future) working force to be effective in incorporating the different transitions we are facing, might be the missing link in getting the real change that we need. I have found very little research on this topic, although this "people factor" is just as important as the "technical factor", in speeding up transitions. What do students learn at universities or training institutes? How is sustainability currently part of our learning programs?

What you show is what you get

The challenges we face are more complex and more urgent than ever. As a consequence, the need for more effective corporate sustainability leaders who can speed up the transition and bring strategies into action is growing. Most of us learn on the job, by listening and exchanging information with our peers. If we want others to see our job as a profession, we should be professionals. This means — even in this very hectic job — investing time in your own personal development, know-how, competencies and skills. "Am I still effective in my job? What competencies do I need? How do I divide my time among the 7 Roles? What can I learn from my peers? How are competencies and roles divided in my team? How is my work/life balance?" These are questions sustainability professionals should ask themselves regularly. And act accordingly.

7 Roles to Create Sustainable Success, is part of my endeavor to stimulate peer-to-peer learning of corporate sustainability leaders around the world. The book, however, covers only a fragment of the current know-how among CSOs. How can we take this further and expand? My journey continues with the founding of the global peer-to-peer learning platform of the Sustainability University Foundation, www.sustainabilityuniversity.org, a social enterprise with the purpose of accelerating sustainability in business. It offers online and off-line learning activities to develop your skills in "getting things done". I hope that this book has inspired you to join me on this journey. It is time to unite in this platform or in another people-oriented learning community. Investing in peer-to-peer learning is crucial if we want to speed up transition.

You are in the lead!

Acknowledgements

"If you want to go fast, go alone. If you want to go far, go together" is an African proverb that certainly holds for this book. There are many people I would like to recognize and thank for making 7 *Roles to Create Sustainable Success* possible. Let me start by thanking my talented and passionate colleagues at NS and all the directors I worked with from 2010, who saw enough in my sustainable dreams to support me. Michiel van Roozendaal and Roger van Boxtel really made a difference to the wind-powered trains. Also, a special thanks to the Sustainability Council, Working Group and my direct team for creating the successes and lessons that are included in the book. I could not have done it without you!

I thank the people who supported the creation of this book. Like the original Dutch book *MVO doe je Zo* (2016), a dear group of female sustainability experts (Birgitta Kramer, Anniek Mauser, Annick Schmeddes, Wineke Haagsma, Anneke Sipkens, Annette van Waning, Esther Verburg, Geanne van Arkel, Tanja Roeleveld and Elfrieke van Galen) who stood by me with valuable tips and moral support. Ellen Weinreb, Todd Cort, Roald Lapperre made several introductions. My former colleague Gilinde van Geldorp made an indispensable contribution with her feedback. Marjolein Baghuis and Chris Verstegen helped in the writing process, as well as the editor Laurens Molegraaf. And Justus Bottenheft used his superb designing talent. Thank you and all the others, like the Consul General of the Netherlands in San Francisco, that helped along the way!

I am very grateful for the inspiring forewords and the incredible valuable input of a large group of experienced CSOs, CSR and sustainability managers and passionate professionals from different parts of the world. Their various contributions have made this a unique book. You can find their stories, insights, lessons learned and tips, throughout the book.

Last but not least, I would like to thank my family and friends, who gave me the time and space to write this book and supported me to the very end.

List of contributors

Kate Rawort n — Economist Senior Visiting Research Associate at Oxford
    University's Environmental Change Institute, Senior Associate at the
    Cambr idge Institute for Sustainability Leadership and author of *Doughnut*
    Economics: Seven Ways to Think Like a 21st Century Economist (2017)
Brian Janous — General Manager of Energy and Sustainability of Microsoft and
    responsible for leading the development and execution of Microsoft's global
    data center energy strategy
Todd Cort — Lecturer Sustainability at Yale School of Management
Janice Lao — Director of the Group Corporate Responsibility and Sustainability at
The Hongkon g & Shanghai Hotels Limited and Owner and Operator of The
    Penins ula Hotels and other luxury real estate assets
Marco Krape s — CEO of Micropower, former VP of Tesla, former Executive VP of
    Rabob ink NA and Co-Chair of the Rabobank's CSR Committee
Esther Verbr rg — VP of Corporate Responsibility at Tommy Hilfiger Global/PVH
    Europ e
Michael Kobori — former VP Sustainability at Levi Strauss & Co. and Chair of the
    company's Sustainability Board; Chief Sustainability Officer at Starbucks
    Coffee Company
Wineke Haagsma — Director Corporate Sustainability of PwC The Netherlands &
    EMEA
Niels van Geenhuizen — Global Leader Sustainable Solutions of Arcadis
Neil Hawkins — former Corporate VP and Chief Sustainability Officer of Dow Inc.
Diane Holdorf — Managing Director Food & Nature, World Business Council
    for Sustainable Development, former CSO and VP of environmental
    stewardship, health and safety of Kellogg Company
Anniek Mauser — Sustainability Director of Unilever Benelux
Darlene Damm — Chair and Principal Faculty of Global Grand Challenges at
    Singularity University
Elfrieke van Galen — Partner at TheRockGroup, Co-Founder and Board Member at
    the Sustainability University Foundation
Marlou Leenders — Global Sustainability Manager of Randstad NV
Franck Dr. Eba — former West Africa CSR Director of SIFCA Group
Geanne van Arkel — Head of Sustainable Development of Interface Europe
Jeroen Cox — Senior Manager Energy & Environment KPN
Eelco Smit — Senior Director Sustainability — Group Sustainability, Philips
    International B.V.
Jacobine Das Gupta — Director Sustainability at DSM
André Veneman — former Corporate Director Sustainability AkzoNobel
Kate Brandt — Google Sustainability Officer
Pia Heidenmark Cook — Chief Sustainability Officer, Ingka Group

Sources and inspiration

Achor, Shawn, *The Happiness Advantage: The Seven Principles of Positive Psychology that Fuel Success and Performance at Work* (2010). Virgin Books.

Bolman, Lee G. (author) and Terrence E. Deal, *Reframing Organizations: Artistry, Choice, and Leadership* (2017). Sixth edition, John Wiley & Sons, Inc.

Chan Kim, W. and Renée Mauborgne, *Blue Ocean Strategy: How to Create Uncontested Market Space and Make the Competition Irrelevant* (2005). Harvard Business Review Press, https://www.blueoceanstrategy.com/.

Das Gupta-Mannak, Jacobine J., *Your Customers Want your Products to be Green: Best Practices of European Sustainability Leaders* (2011). Das Gupta-Mannak.

Hart, Stuart L. and Mark B. Milstein, "Creating Sustainable Value," *Academy of Management Executive*, 17. no.2 (2003), https://doi.org/10.5465/ame.2003.10025194.

Henderson, Rebecca, Gulati, Ranjay and Michael Tushman (eds), *Leading Sustainable Change: An Organizational Perspective* (2015). Oxford University Press.

Jonker J. and N. Faber, "Business Models for Multiple Value Creation: Exploring Strategic Changes in Organisations Enabling to Address Societal Challenges," in A. Aagaard (ed.), *Sustainable Business Models. Palgrave Studies in Sustainable Business In Association with Future Earth* (2019). Palgrave Macmillan, Cham.

Kelly, Marjory, *Owning Our Future: The Emerging Ownership Revolution, Journeys to a Generative Economy* (2012). Berret-Koehler Publishers.

Kielburger, Craig, Branson Holly and Marc Kielburger, *WEconomy: You Can Find Meaning, Make A Living, and Change the World* (2018). John Wiley & Sons.

Kotter, John P., *Leading Change* (2012). Harvard Business Review Press.

Langert, Bob, *The Battle to Do Good: Inside McDonald's Sustainability Journey* (2019). Emerald Publishing Limited.

Maon, François, Lindgreen, Adam and Valérie Swaen, "Designing and Implementing Corporate Social Responsibility: An Integrative Framework Grounded in Theory and Practice," *Journal of Business Ethics*, 87 (2009): 71-89.

Miller, Kathleen and George Serafeim, "Chief Sustainability Officers: Who Are They and What Do They Do?" in Henderson, Rebecca, Gulati, Ranjay and Michael Tushman (eds), *Leading Sustainable Change: An Organizational Perspective* (2015). Oxford University Press. http://nrs.harvard.edu/urn-3:HUL.InstRepos:13350441.

Moratis, Lars, Melissen Frans and Samuel O. Idowu, *Sustainable Business Models, Principles, Promise, and Practice* (2019). Springer Nature.

Porter, Michael E. and Mark R. Kramer, "Creating Shared Value," *Harvard Business Review*, 89. nos 1-2 (2011): 62-77.

Rampersad, Renitha & Chris Skinner, "Examining the Practice of Corporate Social Responsibility (CSR) in Sub-saharan Africa," *Corporate Ownership and Control*, 12. no.1 (2014):723-732. 10.22495/cocv12i1c8p5.

Raworth, Kate, *Doughnut Economics: Seven Ways to Think Like a 21st-Century Economist* (2017). Random House Business Books.

Visser, Wayne and Crane, Andrew, "Corporate Sustainability and the Individual: Understanding What Drives Sustainability Professionals as Change Agents" (February 25, 2010). Available at SSRN: https://ssrn.com/abstract=1559087.

Websites

www.worldbenchmarkingalliance.org/
www.wbcsd.org/
www.weforum.org/reports/the-global-risks-report-2018
www.sasb.org/
www.fsb-tcfd.org/
www.unglobalcompact.org/
www.globalreporting.org/
www.un.org/sustainabledevelopment/sustainable-development-goals
www.ellenmacarthurfoundation.org/
www.ted.com/talks/simon_sinek_how_great_leaders_inspire_action
www.ted.com/talks/steve_howard_let_s_go_all_in_on_selling_sustainability
www.unilever.com/Images/slp_5-levers-for-change_tcm13-387353_tcm244-409796_en.pdf
about.puma.com/en/sustainability/environment
www.levistrauss.com/wp-content/uploads/2015/03/Full-LCA-Results-Deck-FINAL.pdf

List of figures and tables

Notes

1   http://sustainabilityuniversity.org/
2   E. R. Csagie, R. Wesselink, V. Blok, T. Lans & M. Mulder, "Individual
     competencies for corporate social responsibility: A literature and practice
     perspective," *Journal of Business Ethics*, 135 (2016): 233-252. doi: 10.1007/s10551-
     014-2469-0;
     E. R. Csagie, R. Wesselink, V. Blok & M. Mulder, (Accepted)
     "Contextualizing individual competencies for Managing the Corporate
     Social Responsibility Adaptation process: The Apparent Influence of the
     Business Case Logic," *Business & Society*, vol. 58 issue: 2 (2019) 369-403.
     https://doi.org/10.1177/0007650316676270
3   https://www.thenaturalstep.de/about/interface-case-study/
4   Rob van Tilburg, Rob van Tulder, Mara Francken et al. *Managing the transition
     to a sustainable enterprise*, Lessons from Frontrunner Companies (2013),
     Routledge
5   Avastone's model is available via http://nextstepintegral.org/wp-content/
     uploads/2011/04/Mind-sets-In-Action-McEwen-Schmith.pdf
6   https://sdgcompass.org
7   A.H.J. Nijhof & R.J.M. Jeurissen, "The glass ceiling of corporate social
     responsibility: Consequences of a business case approach towards CSR,"
     International Journal of Sociology and Social Policy, 30, 11/12 (2010): 618-631.
8   V. Kasturi Rangan, Lisa Chase, Sohel Karim, "The Truth about CSR," *Harvard
     Business Review* 93, Jan-February (2015): 40-49
9   Rob van Tilburg, Rob van Tulder, Mara Francken et al. *Managing the transition
     to a sustainable enterprise*, Lessons from Frontrunner Companies (2013),
     Routledge
10   https://orrick.blob.core.windows.net/orrick-cdn/Proxy_Generation_PPAs.pdf
11   For more information, see Interface's 25th Anniversary Sustainability
     Report via https://www.interface.com/US/en-US/sustainability/our-journey-
     en_US
12   https://smallactionsbigdifference.net
13   Rob van Tilburg, Rob van Tulder, Mara Francken et al. *Managing the transition
     to a sustainable enterprise*, Lessons from Frontrunner Companies (2013),
     Routledge
14   https://www.ecovadis.com
15   Sustainable Procurement An introduction for practitioners to sustainable
     procurement in World Bank IPF projects, the World Bank, USA, 2nd edition
     (April 2019), Annex I pp. 33-42
16   https://footprint.wwf.org.uk/#/
17   Steve Coley, "Enduring ideas: The three horizons of growth," *McKinsey
     Quarterly*, December 1, 2009

18   https://net-works.com/

19   https://www.nextwaveplastics.org/

20   https://www.dezeen.com/2019/09/04/lena-pripp-kovac-ikea-circular-interview/

21   spm.ei.columbia.edu/files/2015/06/SPM_Metrics_WhitePaper_1.pdf

22   https://www.greenbiz.com/report/2020-state-green-business-report

23   https://oxfam.org/en/research/journey-sustainable-food
      https://www.behindthebrands.org/company-scorecard/

24   K.E.H. Maas & K.C. Liket, "Social impact measurement: a classification of methods." In R. Burrit (ed.), *Environmental Management Accounting*, Supply Chain Management and Corporate Responsibility Accounting USA: Springer (2011), pp. 171-202

25   D. Ewen, K. Maas, & H. Toxopeus, "The impact of circular economy." in *Handbook of Sustainable Innovation*. Edward Elgar Publishing (2019), pp. 331-349

26   For more information on LCA, see for example: M. Z. Hauschild, R. K. Rosenbaum & S. I. Olsen (eds) *Life Cycle Assessment: Theory and Practice* Switzerland: Springer (2018).

27   For more information on the EU Directive: https://ec.europa.eu/info/business-economy-euro/company-reporting-and-auditing/company-reporting/non-financial-reporting_en

28   For more information on the GRI Reporting Standards: https://www.globalreporting.org/standards

29   For more information on integrated reporting: http://integratedreporting.org/resource/international-ir-framework/

30   For more information/source: http://ghgprotocol.org/sites/default/files/ghgp/standards/ghg-protocol-revised.pdf

31   https://www.weinberg.udel.edu/IIRCiResearchDocuments/2018/11/2018-SP-500-Integrated-Reporting-FINAL-November-2018-1.pdf

32   J. van den Berg, M. C. Zijp, W. J. V. Vermeulen & S. Witjes, "Identifying change agent types and its implications for corporate sustainability integration based on worldviews and contextual factors," *Journal of Cleaner Production* (2019), doi:10.1016/j.jclepro.2019.04.272

33   As described by the corporate analyst Marjorie Kelly —there are five key design traits that profoundly shape what every business can do and be in the world: its purpose, governance, networks, ownership and finance

34   From the work of Marjorie Kelly, especially her 2012 book, *Owning Our Future*

35   Eghe Osagie, HAN University of Applied Sciences, Nijmegen: http://www.mmulder.nl/wp-content/uploads/2011/11/Osagie-Eghe-2015-Individual-Competencies-for-Corporate-Social-Responsibility-A-Literature-and-Practice-Perspective.pdf

About the Author

After obtaining a business degree at Nyenrode University, I graduated in 1992, as a Master of International Relations with a focus on Energy Markets, Environment and Technology, at the Johns Hopkins University, SAIS in Washington DC. After several years of working as a consultant in energy and sustainable energy solutions, I became co-owner and CEO of a consultancy business in energy procurement and management. In 2003, I joined the NS as Chief Procurement Officer. After a commercial position as Head of Portfolio Management and Innovation, I was appointed the first Chief Sustainability Officer (CSO) of NS in 2010. Working together with my peers and colleagues to make NS a climate-neutral, circular and inclusive company has been the most inspiring and challenging phase in my career. In 2014 I was rewarded for achieved results, when I was awarded national CSR manager of the year. The next year I also entered the "Sustainable Top 100" of a national newspaper at number 51, to climb up to position 11 by 2017, the same year that the trains ran on 100% wind power. The jury report highlighted my innovative work on sustainability reporting and renewable energy procurement. I believe in the power of business to accelerate transition to a sustainable world as well as the power of peer-to-peer learning. In February 2019, I left my job at NS to boost my activities in the field of empowering sustainability professionals, such as the writing of the book, *7 Roles to Create Sustainable Success*, which is an English translation of my acclaimed Dutch book, *MVO doe je Zo*. For the book I worked together with other CSOs, who have contributed their experiences and practices. Besides being a practical guide for sustainability professionals, *7 Roles to Create Sustainable Success* is — like the Dutch version — also suited as a text book for universities. In 2019, I co-founded with Elfrieke van Galen, the Sustainability University Foundation, a global platform for sustainability professionals with on and off-line peer-to-peer learning activities and research. Working with students and developing new knowledge is one of my key drivers. I do this by guest lecturing at several international universities, like Yale School of Management, Nyenrode University and the University of Amsterdam, and by holding several non-executive positions such as Chairman of the Supervisory Board of Utrecht Science Park and member of the Advisory Board for Business Administration at Radboud University.

 https://7roles.com

Linkedin https://www.linkedin.com/in/carolawijdoogen

✉ carola@7roles.com

printed on 120 g/m²
Munken Kristall 1.13
FSC Mix Credit paper